Be Blesséd

Denise Dumars

New Page Books
A Division of The Career Press, Inc.
Franklin Lakes, NJ

Copyright © 2006 by Denise Dumars

All rights reserved under the Pan-American and International Copyright Conventions. This book may not be reproduced, in whole or in part, in any form or by any means electronic or mechanical, including photocopying, recording, or by any information storage and retrieval system now known or hereafter invented, without written permission from the publisher, The Career Press.

BE BLESSED
EDITED BY JODI BRANDON
TYPESET BY GINA TALUCCI
Cover design by Cheryl Cohan Finbow
Printed in the U.S.A. by Book-mart Press

To order this title, please call toll-free 1-800-CAREER-1 (NJ and Canada: 201-848-0310) to order using VISA or MasterCard, or for further information on books from Career Press.

CAREER PRESS

New Page Books

The Career Press, Inc., 3 Tice Road, PO Box 687,
Franklin Lakes, NJ 07417
www.careerpress.com
www.newpagebooks.com

Library of Congress Cataloging-in-Publication Data

Information available upon request

To Dan Hooker,
a Sage if there
ever was one.

Acknowledgments

There are not words enough to say or green apple martinis enough to repay the kind deeds and wise words of my co-founders of the Iseum of Isis Paedusis, Rev. Lori Nyx and Rev. Stephania Ebony. For their love, patience, and advice I am in their eternal debt. More thanks go to Melody Friend of Temple Eclectica and Laura Sedgwick of Hygeia's Bowl for their support, friendship, and healing.

Similarly, I am humbled by the respect and wise words of our own "Barbara-Yaga," Dr. Barbara Ardinger, who has inspired me to greater confidence in myself as a professor and a writer—no mean feat!

To Dan Hooker of the Ashley Grayson Literary Agency: well, the Fates were never kinder to me than when you became my agent and my friend. And to Ashley and Carolyn Grayson: thanks ever so much for allowing this crazy pagan chick into your office! And to Michael Pye (wacket) of New Page books: You rock, dude.

And thanks to Francisco Arcaute, for introducing me to the real magick of Mexico while writing screenplays, taking photos, and talking to cats. I couldn't have written this book without you.

Contents

Introduction — 11

Chapter 1: Greeting the Sun — 15
Greeting the morning with magickal and spiritual exercises that set the stage for a positive and successful day ahead.

Chapter 2: Self-Esteem for Life — 31
Why it is important to understand self-esteem as a way of enhancing magick and honoring the creators.

Chapter 3: Mindfulness — 51
Being in the moment and why it is necessary to spiritual development as well as personal effectiveness and safety in daily life.

Chapter 4: Dialogues With Deities: How to Talk to a God   63

Suggestions for how to approach, honor, and appeal to a variety of pagan deities from world cultures; in addition, there are guided meditations that may be recorded for personal use and a do-it-yourself guide to creating one's own guided imagery.

Chapter 5: That 4-Letter Word: Work   99

How spirituality and magick can improve your effectiveness at work and help create a positive and creative workplace environment.

Chapter 6: In Sickness and in Health: Yours and Others   113

Ways of coping and healing for yourself and for others who request it.

Chapter 7: Everyday Magick   129

Simple ways to practice magick on a daily basis for the purpose of honing one's skills and developing discipline in the magickal arts.

Chapter 8: And a Good Night to All   177

Prayers and rites for relaxation and a sound, safe night's sleep.

Coda: Physician, Heal Thyself   189

Appendix I: Affirmations Express   195
*A quick reference to the most important
affirmations in the text as well as those
not covered by their own chapters.*

Appendix II: Products and Services   205
*Where to find products and services
mentioned in the book.*

Appendix III: References   215
A full bibliography of sources mentioned in the text.

Index   219

About the Author   223

Introduction

Practicing our beliefs on a daily basis is an excellent goal, but it is also something we may need help with. How to fit some small spiritual element into our busy days can be a challenge. Indeed, many of us are turning into "seasonal pagans," celebrating the major sabbats but not practicing our religion actively throughout the year on a regular basis. But most of us want more; most of us want that connection with Deity in our everyday lives.

Our religion is unusual in that it has two distinct aspects: spirituality and the practice of magick. Magick helps us achieve our personal goals and work for the greater good, but spirituality is an integral part of who we are, and affects us and our relationship with the cosmos on a continuing basis.

Magick takes practice—just as playing the piano does. Even Alicia Keys has to practice, and so do aspiring witches and mages. High Priestess Stephania Ebony says we should practice magick daily, just as I practiced the piano daily when I was a young girl. I figure that if my unruly junior high self could practice the piano on a daily basis, then as an adult I should be able to fit something as valuable as practicing my spirituality into my everyday life!

Though I didn't realize it then, the genesis of this book occurred some years ago, when I worked on a public library reference desk. At the time I often found myself squiring readers to shelves full of books of "daily devotions"—prayers, meditations, affirmations, and so on—that are abundant for followers of Christianity, Judaism, Islam, Buddhism, and other traditional faiths. Clearly, the sheer numbers of people who asked for them proved their value. But few such books exist for modern pagans, Wiccans, and those who follow other magico/religious systems. Certainly there is a need for such books.

The thesis of this book is that, as busy people, we need a way to access Deity and practice magick each day, every day. A good way to start is to have a guide—a book that enables the individual faced with the frenetic pace of the 21st century to practice what he or she preaches on a regular basis.

You don't need to go out and buy a ton of supplies for any of the practices in here, nor do you have to wait for a specific season, day, or phase of the moon. Many other books require such actions, and they should be consulted for seasonal rituals, spells, and more elaborate practices. Also, this book is NOT a "quick and dirty" shortcut to the elaborate practice of ritual and study that our beliefs demand. Rather, it is a guide to improving such practices by integrating aspects of them into our daily lives, or what Dr. Barbara Ardinger calls, in her eponymous book, "practicing the presence of the goddess."

I would suggest reading this book in its entirety first, then turning to each specific section as needed. Hopefully some of the practices herein will become daily rituals with the affirmations committed to memory. It is my hope that by incorporating these ideas into everyday life, the reader will find the practice of our religion to be an enduring source of wisdom, comfort, creativity, and success.

This book will draw in part from examples from my own life and those of others that will serve as guidelines for handling various aspects of life, including relationships, work, health, and community.

Each chapter will begin with assorted appropriate affirmations; separate affirmations are demarcated by spacers, and prayers/poems are titled. I have included a variety of references to various deities in the affirmations and prayers in order to be inclusive as well as to reflect my own practice and how it informs this book; you, of course, should tailor them to your own belief system and your own pantheon. If you have not worked with a specific pantheon you might consider giving it a try. You'll note that many affirmations mention the "God" and "Goddess" generically, as well for those who see view the God/dess form in this fashion.

Try opening the book at random: a bit of bibliomancy to start. Upon what page did your fingers alight? Start there.

Also, each chapter allows the reader to modify and create his or her own "ways of wyrd." There is no dogma here: only a guidebook to assist the individual in taking the road, as Robert Frost would say, less traveled.

Enjoy.

Rev. Denise "Dion-Isis" Dumars
Manhattan Beach, California
Harvest Moon, 2005

Chapter 1

Greeting the Sun

Affirmations

To Say Upon Arising

Arise, Apollo, Arise. Your admirer, your herald, is here. Arise and greet the day.

※

I face the day with joy; I greet the God/dess as I greet the day.

※

I thank the gods for this day.

Morning Prayer

I am born of earth and sky
I awaken with the morning dew and sunray
I hold my arms out to embrace the world
I reach for the spark of life divine;
I am dust and water walking.

I have always liked the idea of morning matins, even though I was not raised Catholic. Somehow the idea of morning prayers really resonates with me, probably because I need all the prayers I can get just to get out of bed in the morning! I mean, there are truly some days when I feel that I'm "dust and water walking." That famous line, spoken by the resurrected Osiris in Egyptian mythology, is taken from a document variously called *The Egyptian Book of the Dead*, *The Book of Coming Forth by Day*, or, as Normandi Ellis calls it, most appropriately, *Awakening Osiris*. Many of us feel each morning like Osiris trying to literally pull himself together and come back from the dead! Osiris, I feel your pain, as do most of us who aren't "morning people."

There are a variety of spiritual and magickal ways to start your day. Start with one of the previous affirmations to awaken yourself spiritually, and then "wake up" your body with the following.

Chi Gong Stretches

This is something you do, not something you say. Most people can do these, even those with disabilities. Though the exercises are described as being performed in the standard chi gong standing position, they may be done while seated for those who cannot stand. I have Melody Friend of Temple Eclectica to thank for sharing these exercises during one of her excellent classes.

To begin, while standing, move each leg to one side so that your feet are about shoulder-width apart. Turn your feet inward slightly, so that you are a bit pigeon-toed. Relax your knees and let them bend a little. Now you are in the standard chi gong standing position.

If you cannot stand, sit on the edge of a firm chair, sofa, or on a stool so that the back of your chair will not be in the way as you do these exercises.

Each of the exercises gets eight repetitions.

Exercise One: Arms at sides, swing them back and forth loosely. It sounds easy, but remember to relax your shoulders while you're doing it. The arms should swing freely, not be "controlled" by the shoulder muscles.

Exercise Two: Swing arms side to side across body and up slightly slowly and carefully. Breathe deeply. Relax.

Exercise Three: Repeat the swinging side-to-side motion of your arms, only this time, as they swing out to the sides, raise them higher.

Exercise Four: Now move arms in a similar motion as before, only this time going all the way around in a circle, alternating deosil and widdershins positions. Remember to do so slowly and thoughtfully; check your posture.

Exercise Five: Swing arms around your body, slapping your back with one hand and your chest with the other. The idea is to "wake up" your lungs and kidneys. If you wish, you may bend over and continue this motion up and down your body, to "wake up" everything else as well! It's kind of fun to "slap" yourself awake, I think.

Exercise Six: Hold arms down to your sides, and raise fingers on each hand as though you had a basketball in each one. Turn your hands in and out, keeping upper arms straight. (It's harder than it sounds.)

Exercise Seven: Make "snake arms." Move right arm upward sinuously, then down, then meet the left arm and do the same, then alternate. Watch each arm as you move; try to take a breath as you raise and lower each arm slowly and gracefully.

Exercise Eight: Stand tall but relaxed. Close your eyes and imagine you are standing beneath a cleansing waterfall. Count slowly to eight, and you're done.

These exercises may be repeated at bedtime. The number eight is considered lucky in Chinese lore, which is why it is important here. After you have become accustomed to doing the exercises, you may increase the number of repetitions and add your own modifications, but do not change each basic exercise; just add to it if you wish. I recommend consulting a chi gong or Tai Chi book or class for more in-depth exercises if you wish. I add the few Pilates exercises I can do, and I also highly recommend Pilates training for those with back problems or those who would like to avoid having back problems! But whatever exercise you choose, doing even a few minutes' worth in the morning will help you wake up and feel better physically, mentally, and spiritually.

Ritual Bathing

I'm not a bath person; I'm a shower person. So while using my sacred shower gel (You think I'm kidding? Raven's Flight makes "Before the Rite" shower gel that is fabulous.) or my hyssop soap, which was sacred to the Egyptians and other people of Biblical times, I say the following, either aloud or to myself:

Pure, pure, I am pure. I stand pure in the light of Isis.

For a longer version of this cleansing prayer utilized by Isians, see deTraci Regula's *The Mysteries of Isis*. Purity was an important aspect of most religious and magickal work in ancient times; the Egyptians have no exclusive patent on this idea. In the days of the pagan religions bathing wasn't as easy or convenient as it is now, and the concept of "purity" usually culminated in a ritual bath. People would purify themselves before ritual by praying; abstaining from certain foods, alcohol, drugs, and sex; and finally, just before the rite, bathing. We have the luxury of everyday purification, so why not start the day this way?

Other purity prayers to say while bathing or afterward:

Purified am I by these waters; I am clean in the eyes of the gods.

☙

Omio, Yemaya. The waters of your womb surround me, cleanse me, purify me.

☙

As Venus was born of the waters, so am I reborn.

> *Stripped of all negativity, I begin clean and pure in the eyes of the Lord and Lady.*

Sometimes I also say the simple chant from the song "Yemaya Assessu" from the album *Satsang: a Meditation in Song and Silence* by Deva Premal and Miten. It consists of a few Yoruban words and an easy melody to remember. Give it a try or write your own chant for your favorite water deity.

If I'm in pain or feeling poorly, I also chant The Isis Prayer:

> *Isis attend me; Isis mend me.*

For more on the uses of this very simple and direct prayer, see Chapter 6. If you have pain on arising I would also recommend using a lavender-based shower gel, bath salts, and/or shampoo; Avalon Organics has a whole line of organic lavender bath products available from Trader Joe's, Whole Foods, and many other sources. I sometimes put some lavender and rosemary oil together in the diffuser so that I feel both alert and relaxed when I leave for work, or some niaouli if I'm worried about anything I may face during the day ahead.

Bath of the Four Elements Plus One

This is a somewhat more formal version of my previous, basic suggestion. Get some lavender bath salts, or plain Epsom salts if you prefer an unscented bath. Usually a cupful to a bathtub is about right, or follow the directions on the commercial product. If showering, get one of those plastic beach buckets and simply put the salts in it and then fill with hot water while in the shower and pour it over yourself, a little at a time.

So far we've got earth (salts) and water. For air and fire, you'll need an oil warming diffuser, a tea candle, and some essential oil. Good morning oils include lavender, rosemary, geranium, basil, or peppermint. Put some oil and water into the diffuser and light the tea candle. Alternately, you can burn a stick of incense and light a candle if you prefer.

Now for the fifth element; sorry, guys, but it's not Milla Jovovich! Before stepping into the bath or shower, take three deep breaths, breathing from the diaphragm. Do so again after you emerge from the bath. This is the kind of breathing you have to practice to get right; start by studying the first steps toward pranic breathing as discussed in the mindfulness chapter (Chapter 3). Imagine with each breath that you are cleansing and purifying your spirit while inhaling and exhaling.

While shaving, putting on make-up, styling your hair, or just checking your outfit before you leave for work, say this next short prayer. It is very important, as we will see in the self-esteem chapter (Chapter 2).

To say before the mirror:

I am beautiful and loved.

Say it. Mean it. Revise it any way you want, but don't step out from in front of that mirror without saying it at least three times!

Greeting the Gods

Now that you are awake and "purified," it is the perfect time to greet your patron deities. Some prefer to wake up and go to sleep with the same deities in mind; others prefer to say hello at the proper time of day. For example, a follower of a solar deity such as Sekhmet may wish to address her in the morning, and a follower of a lunar deity such as Thoth might prefer to greet that deity in the evening. Think about how you relate to your patron god or goddess, and what symbols in nature relate to that deity. Because solar and lunar magick are so powerful and these symbols so integral to our beliefs, do not hesitate to "say hello" to solar and lunar deities as appropriate. Here is an appropriately solar prayer for Sekhmet:

Sekhmet of the Sun

Sekhmet Sekhem
Sekhmet of the sun,
Fire of the eye of Ra,
Rise thou in strength, in power,
As energetic as a solar flare
As bright as the rays of Sol, our star
Illuminate my path today
As I, your (son/daughter), go forth
Into the world to do your good works.
Sa sekhem, Sekhmet,
Sa sekhem!

It is best to create your own prayer or affirmations for your personal deity. I will have an example of a prayer to a lunar deity (Thoth) in Chapter 8.

For That SAD Person

Now, I like to joke around a lot in my books, but Seasonal Affective Disorder (SAD) is no laughing matter. People with this disorder get profoundly depressed when the weather turns cloudy and the days become shorter. I have a friend who has this disorder and I can tell you that she craves sunshine the way some people crave Krispy Kreme doughnuts.

Now, I know what you're thinking: California, land of eternal sunshine. Well, here in the coastal area, thanks to our meteorological phenomena, which have been dubbed a "couple"—Onshore Flo and Coastal Eddie—there are sometimes whole months out of the year when we wake up to overcast or foggy skies. Sometimes, therefore, the sun doesn't come through until late in the afternoon—just in time for our sea breeze off the Pacific to pick up, bringing in—you guessed it—more low clouds and fog. You may have heard the term *June gloom*, which was coined to cover what happens here when the rest of the country is just starting to get warm and sunny.

So, what to do? Well, doctors recommend getting a full-spectrum light bulb, which mimics natural sunlight, for home and office. But because this is a disorder mainly of emotional effects, I wonder if there isn't a spiritual dimension to it as well. Here is an exercise to do when you find your sunshine hasn't quite broken through the clouds when you get up in the morning.

Do some pranic breathing exercises (see Chapter 3), and, if you feel motivated enough, do your stretches. If not, then do this exercise first.

Wearing something comfortable (keep the jammies on) or—why not—going skyclad, stand in a place where you can see where the sun is supposed to be (you can, uh, keep the curtains closed if you're skyclad). Spread your arms wide, really stretching your pectorals. Then raise your arms over your head and, finally, lower your elbows to your sides but keep your hands open, facing the sun. Now say this prayer:

Helios, Rise

Helios, rise;
Rise, oh star of day,
Rise, and shine upon me
Rise, and spread your starry radiance
Deep within my heart.
Helios, rise;
Rise for me, rise through me.

Shake out your arms and hands, then spread them wide again. Close your eyes, and feel the rays of the sun warming your heart. Use your imagination as much as you need to until you really *feel* a warming sensation. Then open your eyes, and thank the sun. When you find yourself starting to get "blue" again, conjure up that bright sunshine in your heart and feel its warmth flowing through you, easing out that depressing color and initiating a sparkling radiance of full-spectrum sunlight.

Other Ways to Up the Ante for a Successful Day

Stir some cinnamon into your coffee for a prosperous day. I've gotten into the habit of sprinkling cinnamon in the coffee filter even before I put the coffee in. If you're not a coffee drinker, stir some ginger into your tea or drink chai, which is loaded with "prosperity" spices.

Before leaving, use a scent that makes sense (bad pun; sorry) for whatever you're doing. For example, I have several Yardley fragrances; though these are artificial scents that don't have magickal powers, they do evoke certain reactions, as smell is the faculty most linked to memory. For example, I could use rose to endear myself to others; orange blossom to "sweeten" any business deal; magnolia to help others remember me; and lavender to feel relaxed and confident. I have that wonderful ginger body crème from Origins that Oprah loves so much; I also have a ginger body spray and bath gel. Ginger is for prosperity, and a gingery cologne smells great on both men and women.

Color is another way to step out the door with more confidence. If you'll be dealing with the boss or anyone in a higher position than yourself then try to wear something with royal blue or royal purple in it, such as a tie, blouse, or scarf. These colors are called "royal" for a reason: They are the traditional colors of kings, and they operate at a higher frequency than other colors and so they increase your chances of being seen as "royalty" (or at least upper management). Red is another power color; the red power tie is a classic and, as red is the color of Catholic cardinals, it also represents a high spiritual status, which seems ironic for such as "carnal" color. I'll discuss some of these issues more in the "work" chapter (Chapter 5).

Do not wear red or orange, however, if you have pain and inflammation or are seething with anger about the lack of a pay raise or some other such issue! Green, blue, or pale pink will calm you.

Travel Protection

Most of us don't work from home, so most of us travel at least five days per week—usually by car. And, wow! Do our cars needs protection! The following affirmation was created after I'd had an auto accident. Athena, as a goddess of wisdom, is an air goddess. She is also a war goddess who is often depicted wearing a helmet and armor, and as such is well prepared to protect our cars from whatever scary stuff is out there. It's easy to find a photo of Athena on the Internet or in reference books, and many shops carry small reproductions of statues of Athena, as does Sacred Source. It wouldn't hurt to have one in your car or home.

Auto Protection Affirmations

Athena, protect my car. Let other drivers see me and respect me.
Athena, help me drive defensively.
Athena, armor my car and keep all who ride in it safe.

Greeting the Sun

On the road try some deep breathing to keep your cool. You may want to say the following to yourself if you drive long distances or have to drive late at night:

Like the triform God/dess, I see all around me, am alert to all hazards, and am immune to all distractions.

Again, if you drive long distances or are driving late at night, you need to be alert. Please don't put on somnolent classical music or that "smooth jazz" station. If you can't stand rock music or another raucous, lively format, try getting some of the louder Middle Eastern tapes. All that wailing and crashing of cymbals will keep you awake for sure, and the deities seem to love it.

Or then again, if you're into the Norse pantheon, Wagner works, too.

If you take public transportation, then a special form of protection may be needed as well—namely, protection from the others on the same bus, train, or subway! Sometimes a charm is in order; I favor the idea of a piece of rose quartz in a flannel bag to be kept in one's pocket or purse so that others will look kindly on you instead of looking at you as a potential mugging victim. Don't forget to shield yourself once you're safely seated, and "brush" your aura to cleanse it once you get home or have a friend or family member smudge you with sage or a similar herb. It is my hope that, eventually, when it is possible for the majority of us to take public transportation where we need to go, that such worries will decrease.

Air Travel

Whenever I'm on a plane—which isn't nearly often enough, I feel—I do the following: Before its ascent I close my eyes and visualize the wings of Isis lifting the plane and carrying it safely to its destination, then setting it down gently again. I find nowadays when I do this that my vision of Isis is that of the *kite*, a bird that was equated with the goddess. If we sit on the tarmac for a while, I also visualize the other planes I can see being protected and carried by Isis's wings.

The last time I flew I noticed my visualization had changed again. Now the winged creature that lifted us aloft seemed to look more similar to the Horus falcon. Perhaps in this post–9/11 world the more militaristic Horus falcon adds an extra dimension of security to the flight.

A lot of people dislike flying, and fear it. Statistically speaking, you're far safer getting on that plane than you are getting into your car each morning, but, as we all know, fears aren't necessarily rational. Try the preceding Isis visualization each time you fly if you feel nervous. Add whatever embellishments you like—perhaps an Isian "Mae West" made of Isis's wings strapped around your chest as an astral flotation device, or any other idea that makes you feel safe.

Some people wear special amulets while traveling. An Eye of Horus as a necklace, bracelet, or ring is certainly a good idea and is not likely to get confiscated at the gate.

I am told that in some parts of Latin America people cross themselves, thank the Virgin, and applaud when the plane lands safely. Maybe we ought to do something similar as well!

Now your day has begun. Step out of the house and into the world with a smile. You are powerful; you are god/dess. Don't hide your light under a bushel (whatever that means). Be proud. You deserve to be.

Chapter 2

Self-Esteem for Life

Affirmations

I believe in myself and my vision.

☙❧

Say before a mirror three times or as many times as you need to for it to sink in:

I am beautiful and loved.

☙❧

Oh, that again! Yes, that again. I mentioned it in Chapter 1 and I'll keep mentioning it until you say it and mean it! Self-esteem is so very important that I can't emphasize it enough. Some might say that it is the most powerful magick of all. After all, it will get you ahead in the mundane world and in the magickal one; what other characteristic does both?

Here's another affirmation:

I am loved by the goddess and the god.

(Whenever I say "goddess and/or god" you may substitute your own favorite deities if you wish.)

I am beautiful and loved.

Memorize it. Say it when you are getting ready for work, getting ready for a date, and whenever you look in the mirror, even if it's just while washing your hands.

More affirmations:

I am a reflection of the God/dess.

༶

I am blessed; I am doing the gods' work.

༶

The power of the gods flows through my body.

༶

In living my life, I honor the gods.

༶

Prayers for Self-Esteem

Made of God and Goddess

I am made of such as stars are made,
I am part and parcel of the gods,
These hands, these feet, these arms, these legs
Do the god/desses' work,
Connected to the firmament,
Connected to the cosmos,
I am made of God and Goddess,
I am shining starstuff speaking,
See me, hear me, know me,
I walk with gods,
I am god/dess.

Beauty's Reign

I hear men speak of beauty
As though she were a queen
But every woman is beautiful
Every woman reigns supreme.
So hold high your head majestic
And walk with regal glide
And be a benevolent ruler…
If just a little bit snide!

Now I am going to talk about putting yourself first. I don't mean being selfish, but rather looking out for your own best interests—in this case, your self-esteem. Without it, you literally have nothing. Your own self-image has a tremendous amount of power. You are the one who decides how others see you, and you're a magickian, remember? So you can change a negative self-image to a positive one and others will follow suit.

Self-esteem is not about being stuck-up or vain. It is about owning your own uniqueness, which implies the fact that you are a reflection of the gods and are therefore innately worthy of self-esteem. In fact, to have low self-esteem could be thought of as an insult to the gods! In order to "be the best you can be" and to honor the deities, you must possess self-esteem. Now, here's an example:

The Vanishing American

If possible, look up an obscure little fantasy story called "The Vanishing American" by the late Charles Beaumont, who may be known to you as the writer of several of the best original *Twilight Zone* episodes. In the story a meek little man follows the same daily routine for so long that he literally becomes invisible to those around him. Once he realizes that he can't be seen by others, he takes the opportunity to do something he's wanted to do since he was a child: climb onto one of the stone lions outside the New York Public Library. He does so and, to his amazement, hears people laughing. He looks around to see some of them pointing at him—

he's visible again! And all because he did something out of the ordinary.

Break your routine. Do something different. Be just a little bit unpredictable. Be mysterious. People will respect you more, believe it or not. Demand to be heard, to be seen, to be acknowledged and given your due. Don't let anyone treat you as though you were invisible—and some people will do so, if given the chance. Speak up for yourself. Don't let the waiter nearly knock you over to wait on the sweet young thing across the room first. Call the maitre d'. Explain the situation. Say, for example, that you are scooping out the place as a possible lunch destination for your business deals and that you have some very important clients. Say that you don't appreciate the rudeness you have received or the preferential treatment certain others have been getting. Say that you are considering crossing this location off your list. Then watch the maitre d' quail and grovel. It's a lot of fun; trust me on this one.

It's fun to keep 'em guessing. If people at work are taking you for granted, or "forget" to invite you to a special birthday lunch or golf date, or "forget" to give you your cost of living raise when it is due, it's time for a makeover. Dye your hair a different color suddenly; then just as suddenly a week or so later, dye it back to its usual color. Vary your clothing style; if you wear flowery dresses, switch off to a tailored suit. If you're a guy and you dress conservatively, wear a brightly colored shirt once a week—but not always on the same day of the week. Give no explanation for these changes, or even acknowledge that there's anything different about yourself. Then gracefully remind the boss and coworkers that, yes, you'd love to come to Luis's birthday lunch and yes, Wilma and Rachana got their cost-of-living raises on their checks but payroll must have made a mistake with yours.

And by all means stop allowing yourself to be tried in the court of public opinion. You've committed no crime just because you're not as thin, rich, tall, or whatever as the next person. Lead by example; if you are tolerant then others will be more inclined to be so too.

We are too hung up, by the way, on physical beauty—in case you hadn't noticed! Victorian Londoners—another vain bunch—learned that even the "Elephant Man" had a beautiful mind and soul, and, believe me, our society could use a good awakening in that area. A good spiritual exercise for those who are too focused on our culture's ideal of physical beauty might include a viewing of the David Lynch film about this eminent Victorian or any other film—such as *Mask* or *Smile*—that deals with the subject of physical deformity or "ugliness." It is a lesson in compassion well learned.

And learn the one Wiccan rede that 21st-century pagans seem to have forgotten: *Know when to be silent.* Yes, especially you teenagers who demand to wear your pentacles to parochial school and blab about your Craft to anyone who'll listen—and some who probably won't. Remember: As pagans we do not proselytize. Let's take the Jerry Springer confess-all attitude and throw it in the trash where those people belong. Everyone in the world does not need to know your private business. So stop wearing that dirty linen where everyone can see it, and present a positive face that others can see as a role model. Giving people reasons to pigeonhole or alienate you will not help your self-esteem.

Then just imagine when they find out that their role model is a pagan! Keep silent when it is prudent to do so; there are "peasants with torches" out there, so remember: The life you save may be your own.

However, you should also stand up for yourself! Be polite, but don't let others exclude you from important work events, family events, or social events just because they know you're pagan. For example, don't let others "assume" that you don't want to go to the Christmas party just because you're not Christian. And yes, do go to the spa with the rest of the girls even if it means that as a size 12 you're getting undressed with a bunch of size 2s or vice versa. Somehow, without our "armor" on we all seem equal.

Going through these exercises will help insure that you don't become a "vanishing American," because being invisible, although a good thing at times, will never get you the best seat in the house—not to mention the Senate!

Sonrisa

Sonrisa is the Spanish word for smile. It sounds a little bit like "sunrise," which I think is nicely serendipitous. In Mexico, as in many other countries, it is customary to smile and greet the proprietor of a store, restaurant, or public building upon entering. On my recent trip to Mexico City, needless to say while sightseeing and shopping I went into a great number of shops, museums, restaurants, and the like. I smiled and greeted a lot of people. Just walking down the street, in fact, I smiled and spoke to dozens of people. I guess I pretty much had a smile on my face most of the time, now that I look back on it. And you know what? My usually somewhat stern mien began to take on a naturally happier expression. The more I smiled, the more I wanted to smile, and the better I felt. Coming back to L.A., where often times no one will speak to you even if you speak to him or her first, I felt my smile slipping. So I began reminding myself to smile. And as on my trip, I started to feel more positive. Give it a try.

And there's nothing wrong with having good manners and greeting folks, either.

There are many other ways to raise your self-esteem. Doing "good works" is a classic way to do so. What does this mean to pagans? Perhaps helping our your fellow pagans in need. Perhaps volunteering time or giving money to a charity that you believe in; some suggestions that fit in with our belief systems include environmental groups, animal welfare groups, children's advocacy groups, hospitals and hospices, women's and children's shelters, and groups that protect our rights to speak and worship as we please, such as the ACLU. Ask your pagan friends for the names of their favorite charities.

But let's put on our own oxygen mask first before helping others on with theirs, okay? Take stock of your physical body. Unlike some other more traditional religions, pagans do not believe that the body is something to deny or somehow "rise above," but rather is a gift from the gods to be celebrated. You've no doubt heard the saying "during the week my body is a temple; on the weekends, it's an amusement park." Well, that wouldn't be so bad if we didn't treat our bodies as garbage dumps most of the time. What do you eat? Do you eat a balanced diet or live on potato chips and soda pop? Do you follow fad diets or do you watch your weight by eating sensibly and exercising? What we put into our bodies is important. Okay, so we all need to have a Coke once in a while and, now that they've decided that chocolate and red wine are good for us, we can put those back on our grocery lists. But overindulging in sugar, salt, fat, alcohol, or using dangerous drugs is treating your body as a garbage dump, not the gift from the gods that it is. Now, I'm not advocating throwing out all the goodies in the house and putting a padlock on the refrigerator, I'm talking about making small steps toward a healthy lifestyle.

Today, throw out one item of junk food, and do your chi gong exercises or begin doing whatever exercise your doctor has recommended. I just went and threw out the salt and vinegar potato chips, so there! If you must eat fast food, pick sensible choices such as grilled chicken or salads, which are available now at almost any fast food chain. And don't supersize anything—not even diet soda. The chemicals in diet soda are worse for you than sugar, so drink water or iced tea and have a small, sugared soda once in a while to treat yourself. (If you're not diabetic, that is!) I would suggest Mexican Coke, which is available in the United States in Latino markets. Why? It's sweetened with sugar, which is sucrose, not corn syrup, which is fructose. Food products sweetened with corn syrup are much more likely to cause "sugar shock" to the body and also make you crave more of it! Drink a glass of water on arising and remind yourself throughout the day to drink a glass every few hours. The next time you go through the kitchen, throw out items that contain corn syrup. You might just find your "sugar" cravings begin to wane.

See your doctor and dentist. Try if at all possible to keep your teeth! Do not eschew traditional allopathic doctors for holistic practitioners; both have important ways of maintaining our good health, and it is prudent to learn which type of medicine is best for a particular ailment. In other words, homeopathy is not going to set a broken bone, though once the doctor has set it you might want to drink boneset tea to hurry the healing process!

Improve your appearance any way you wish that is not harmful to your health. Yes, I dye my hair; yes, I wear make-up; but that doesn't mean you have to. Looking neat, clean, and healthy is the best way to feel good about your looks. Having your stomach stapled and your breasts augmented just to look better are not healthy ways of maintaining your weight and your looks, no matter what our society says about plastic surgery.

Not that I'm minimizing our society's focus on looks or how hard that is on us. You might be surprised to learn that, nowadays, in many professions—yes, even my own—youth and good looks appear to be the best ticket to a good job. So it's no wonder I enjoy the fictional depictions of the aged and venerable professors portrayed in the Harry Potter stories and movies. They are, sadly, quite fictitious indeed.

But are there any perqs to aging? Yes, indeed. I'll share a silly story and then I'll tell you more about what they are.

The Ideal Customer

When I was young and went to browse through the cosmetic counters in big department stores, the clerks would always hover over me, frowning as though I were going to steal something. (Maybe it was the Mohawk…or the black lipstick.) Whatever the case, they certainly looked at me as though I couldn't afford anything in their display cases and therefore should just go away as quickly as possible.

My, how the situation has changed! I went into Sephora and was interested in the line of therapeutic cosmetics by Dr. Nicholas Perricone. I explained to the clerk that I didn't want to buy such expensive cosmetics without trying them first, so she gave me samples equal to, oh, the amount of one of those $85 bottles. On another occasion I found myself at Macy's talking to the salesperson at the Burberry counter. We had a lovely conversation about London, and she was more than happy to give me samples—I hadn't asked for any, but she clearly saw me as a monied individual who would buy some Burberry eventually, so she gave me some. Finally, I was as Nordstrom and looking at the Christian Dior when a young lady came over—she didn't even work in that department—and went out of her way to help me get samples of the Dior products I was interested in.

Why the change? Am I really more likely to buy these products than when I was young, or is that just the perception? Why do the clerks now court me, falling all over themselves to give me samples of very expensive lotions and anti-aging potions? I don't know the answer to that, but all I can say is, *Whee*! Give it a try if you're, uh, over 35. Don't be afraid to ask for samples of Dior, Chanel, or other expensive brands. As a person of a certain age you have buying power, or are at least presumed to have it. Now's the time to exercise it. Who knows—if the royalties on this book are good enough, maybe I'll actually go back and buy some of that stuff!

Best of all, it doesn't cost a thing. So hold your head high when you shop—believe it or not, you're now the ideal customer.

Being older, I'm realizing, has other perqs as well—and no, I don't mean senior discounts, although those certainly will be a boon when I get old enough to take advantage of them! So that's in fact one other perq. And you can wear purple (though I'd suggest starting now) and you can hang out with the kids and puppies at the party instead of competing for admiration with the other so-called "adults." You can command respect—brandishing that cane helps, too, and if you have one with a sword in it, even better (though they won't let you on the plane with it).

Now give yourself a great big hug. Right now: Put down the book and do it! Start believing in yourself. Think of other areas of your life that could be improved if your self-esteem was higher. Write them down here:

1. _____
2. _____
3. _____
4. _____
5. _____

And continue if you wish. Now focus on what you wrote. Copy them onto any small pieces of paper you would normally use for petitions to deities or other magickal purposes. For example, if you wrote, "my job," copy it over onto the parchment. Then write across it "better job." Then write across that "excellent job." And so on. Try to feel the magick of this area of your life improving, and so your self-esteem. Where does one end and the other begin? I don't know. It's a chicken-and-egg question. But if you feel better about yourself then others will, too, and good things can happen.

Put your petition under a candle or however you usually work with them. If you do the candle thing, keep the petition there until the candle has been consumed—no, you don't have to leave it lit 24/7; in fact, to do so is dangerous. Snuff it out when you leave the house or go to sleep, and state, "The flame is out but my intent remains" or something similar. When the candle is consumed, don't throw it and the petition into a body of living water, bury it in the yard, or whatever oddly environmentally unfriendly way of disposing of it you may have read before. Instead, burn the petition, seeing the intent rise to the heavens with the smoke, and dispose of the candle glass if it was one of those seven-day candles by washing it out and placing it in the recycling bin, if your city offers them to residents.

But of course, we're not done yet, because just when you think it's safe to go to back to the sauna…

We have large size!

That's what the lady at Richness Fashion in Chinatown always says as I'm walking through one of my favorite malls there.

(A XXX-large is comparable to a size 12 there, by the way.) But that's nothing compared to what happened to my friend recently at a Korean spa.

She goes there frequently and, the last time she did so, someone noticed she had gained a little weight. "You look fat!" said the woman at the check-in desk. "Well, tell me something I don't know," said my friend.

And the story got better from there. One of the other women said to yet more of the Korean ladies, "She got fat! Come look how fat she got!" And they were upon her.

Though she laughed about this story, I wonder what it means culturally. Did the fact that the women acknowledged her weight gain mean that they were putting her down? Were they concerned? Did they just find it funny? I have no idea. But I do know that different cultures look at weight much differently from our own, and, now that our American culture is the most diverse in the world, I suppose it's possible that our viewpoint may change.

Perhaps it's good to have someone notice your weight gain: at least they're noticing you, which is quite the opposite from the norm in our dominant culture, especially here in Los Angeles.

I wonder how things will change: in about 15 years, persons such as myself, who are of primarily non-Hispanic European ancestry, will be in the minority in California. Culture defines size, does it not? I saw recently that the winner of an African beauty contest, one similar to the *Miss America* contest, was 38 years old, was married with four children and wore the equivalent of a size 16. Video of the beauty contest was on TV and she was gorgeous, but of course the anorexic newsreader grimaced as she gave the report.

Courage, people! That's what we need. And I don't mean to just focus on women here. Men, too, are judged on their looks in this society, so to deal with the world's weighty issues, courage is encouraged, so to speak. So please, guys, don't get those ugly hair plugs or those ridiculous calf and pec implants!

All right, guys, have you ever referred to someone as being spineless? That means weak, of course. So here's a prayer for courage and strength that makes reference to the Egyptian Djed pillar:

Strength

I am strong of soul
And core;
The backbone of Osiris
Is my backbone;
The courage of Osiris
Is my courage.
I am a pillar of strength
And celebrate my courage
As a blessed child of the gods.

And if you'd like to continue in this vein, we can go on:

I am a child of Osiris;
Commanding chariot,
I hold my head high.

The backbone of Osiris
Is my backbone,
Is my strength, my courage.
I am born to be strong,
And the courage of Osiris
Lives within me.

The Djed pillar is an Egyptian design meant to represent the stylized backbone of Osiris. It symbolizes strength and courage in the face of impossible odds. Try saying this prayer when you are afraid or someone has made you feel small. Take back your strength and courage, which are the hallmarks of the gods. Visualize your spine as the Djed pillar if you like, or as the backbone of Osiris. Remember that you are your own person, your own Pharoah, if you will, and that you and you alone decide how you think about yourself and how you run your life.

If this seems a bit too martial for you, then consider your spine as a strong stalk of bamboo, as is done in chi gong, and do this visualization, which is similar to one I experienced in a meditation with acupuncturist Laura Sedgwick:

The Strength of Bamboo

Sit down, close your eyes, and take five deep pranic breaths. Imagine a hollow bamboo tube that runs from your navel to your spine. Intersecting it is your spine, another hollow stalk of bamboo. Hold your arms out in front of you, arms circling an imaginary basket filled with strength and courage. Now slowly bring your arms toward your stomach, cradling those qualities and gradually transferring them to the horizontal bamboo tube. Once that tube is full, switch your attention to your spine. See it as a bamboo stalk: very strong, but also very pliable. Bend over, touching the floor, and see yourself as a stalk of bamboo swaying in the wind, but connected to the earth. Then sit back up straight, and stretch your arms high to the sky, feeling connected to the cosmos as well.

Now take that small tube of strength and courage that bisects your spine and fill your spine with its reservoir of those qualities. Stay flexible and pliable; you don't want to become rigid. Think of trees that are blown down in a high wind because they cannot bend, and then think of a grove of bamboo or palm trees swaying in the wind and staying anchored because they can bend.

Do this every day if you need to until you feel more confident. After a while, you should be able to quickly visualize and greet the day with more confidence.

Just think about magick. It takes a lot of moxie to believe that you can manipulate reality to achieve your goals. Talk about self-esteem being absolutely mandatory! So let's try a magickal self-esteem exercise.

The Self-Esteem Spell

Dress as you would for a typical ritual or magickal act. Arrange your altar the way you normally would when you are about to start a ritual or spell. Have spring water, incense, at least one candle, and a small bowl of earth or salt on the altar. Make sure you have done the "I am beautiful and loved" affirmation while getting ready.

Now cast a circle with you wand, athame, sistrum, or whatever you usually use. Say these words while walking the circle:

Strength and magick flow from me
Flow through me
To cast this circle.

Repeat until you have cast the entire circle. Now, stand in the middle of the circle and close your eyes, and breathe normally. Notice what you feel. Do you feel any power surging through you? Don't force it or *try* to imagine it; just feel it. Now, keep your eyes closed and envision the circle as a powerful force field surrounding and protecting the room. Imagine it growing until it reaches from the ground all the way to the ceiling.

Now open your eyes, and approach the altar. Light the candle, feeling your own power flowing from your arm to the candle while lighting it; *you* are the source of the flame. Now light the incense and do the same thing. Place your hand over the water, directing energy into it. Do the same with the salt or earth. Now say:

This is my power.
I now demonstrate
This power and manifest it.
I am powerful
And I know it
And others know it as well.

If you don't like those words you're free to make up your own, but they must have the same meaning. Please do not modify them to make them less strong. Remember that you are not bound by any rules that say it is bad to be proud of who you are or that it is wrong in some way to assert yourself. Those outmoded ideas have no place in this circle.

Now say any prayers or speak to any gods that you wish. When you are done, open the circle by walking around widdershins (counter-clockwise) and using your own power to bring down the shields. End by saying something such as this:

> *My power has created and demarcated this circle.*
> *Let it now be opened, by my will, by my power.*

You might be surprised at how hard this is to do at first. You shouldn't feel that you are draining yourself of energy—the display should eventually feel effortless. But mark my words: Once you've done it a few times, you *will* feel the power and you will find your magickal self-esteem growing.

Now apply that magickal self-esteem in your daily life to even your mundane activities. You'll be amazed at what a difference it makes.

Chapter 3

Mindfulness

Affirmations

Affirmations for Being Here Now

I stand in the light of the gods.

❧

Right here, right now, I am in perfect harmony with my surroundings.

❧

Right here, right now, I am at peace with the world.

❧

Right here, right now, the gods and I are one.

❧

Right here, right now, I focus on one thing at a time.
One thing at a time.
One at a time.
One.

What is mindfulness? Is it the old "chop wood, carry water" idea that everything we do is an act of prayer? Well, yes. But if you prefer a more modern, secular interpretation, you could call it being "on-task." Being on-task means that you're not instant-messaging your girlfriend when you're supposed to be writing that monthly sales report; being on-task means that you truly *are* spotting your buddy when he's lifting weights and not daydreaming about the blonde on the treadmill.

How mindful are you? Do you buy into the modern age's idea of multitasking? Do you talk on your cellphone while you drive, or do other dangerous things such as put on makeup or—and yes, I've seen this many times—read the newspaper? If so, STOP. NOW. For a moment, just stop what you're doing, including reading this book.

Did you stop reading? Really? Good—you're learning! Now here are some more affirmations and meditations on mindfulness.

One more thing: NEVER meditate while driving, okay?

Mindfulness on a daily basis requires practice. Consciously bring your attention back to the task at hand when you feel your mind drifting off toward something else. Are you watching your favorite show while a friend on the phone is pouring out her soul to you? Maybe mindfulness also means putting our priorities in order.

The following is an exercise devised by Melody Friend of Temple Eclectica. It's easy to do and remember. Here goes:

Place your right hand over your heart. Tap your chest gently and repeat:

To be
To be
To be

Start out loud. Then repeat, only softer. Repeat the phrase several times, letting your voice get softer and softer as you go along. Then change the affirmation to *be, be, be*. That's it. Just BE. That's a pretty important thing. Then if you wish you can follow with the more familiar *I Am*. Now sit down and we'll talk about breathing.

The God and the Goddess made us with the ability to have an autonomic nervous system that assures that, unless something goes horribly wrong (which is why we invented the ventilator, which used to be known by the less-than-charming sobriquet *iron lung*), you can breathe without thinking about doing it.

Don't take this ability for granted. Certainly people with asthma don't. I've known many who can tell terrifying stories of what it's like to suddenly be unable to effectively draw air into the lungs. So just because most of us can do it without thinking doesn't mean that we should. So let's think about our breathing, and do some pranic breathing exercises.

Pranic Breathing

To become more mindful, stop and focus on your breathing. True pranic breathing, which means to heal through breath, is a long process to learn and takes a lot of practice. What we're doing here is a simpler version that you can practice. If you wish to go further with it, then see the works of Alan Watts or another practitioner of Zen, dhyana, or chi gong to learn the intricacies of the technique.

Begin by placing your hand on your stomach—actually, just above your stomach in the area that contains what is called the diaphragm. Now breathe in, feeling your stomach inflate. That's right; draw the air into your stomach, filling the lower lungs and pushing down the diaphragm. Now breathe out, all the way, through your mouth, and pull your stomach in. Do this at least three times. Practice by seeing how long you can continue to push air out of the lungs.

Your chest and shoulders should not rise while you are doing pranic breathing. If so, then you are not drawing air into the lower lungs. When you start practicing, you might have someone gently put their hands on your shoulders to make you aware of whether or not you're filling the lower lungs or just the upper and therefore lifting your shoulders. This type of shallow breathing does NOT relax you; in fact, it causes the upper body muscles to contract, and if you're anything at all similar to me, you have enough tension in your shoulders, neck, and upper body already. Do pranic breathing before any meditation session or before performing magick (along with grounding), or just do it to help relax and awaken yourself at the same time.

For me, the hardest aspect of mindfulness has to be the effect that anger has on it. When I am angry, I will make mistakes. I will walk into doors, fall down stairs, or snap at someone who did nothing more than cross my path when I happened to be angry.

Anger is frightening; it is also a survival mechanism, just as pain is. Perhaps you've seen on television a story about a person unlucky enough to be born without pain receptors. As I watched one such show where the frantic parents tried to keep a child born without the ability to feel pain from fatally injuring herself, I realized that pain and anger are gifts, not detriments, for a parent's ability to get angry will help protect his or her child from harm. If you don't believe me, well, let's just say don't play with any baby bears you find in the woods, okay?

It's not a coincidence that Zen meditation often requires that you stay a bit uncomfortable—such as in the traditional lotus position or sitting back on your heels. The discomfort is supposed to keep you awake and on-task. A Zen master may whack his student with a bamboo stick, not to hurt him, but to make him pay attention. Anger and pain do the same thing: They make us pay attention, which is what mindfulness is all about. They are, therefore, survival mechanisms, and should not be ignored any more than a STOP sign or a DON'T FEED THE BEARS sign.

All we have is NOW. Yesterday's news is for wrapping fish; tomorrow's news is yet to be written. Do not ignore anger or pain, or pretend they don't exist. This is especially true for women in our society; we seem to have made great strides toward equality, but still aren't allowed to get angry. Much of our anger is justified; we still make 75 cents for every dollar that a man makes; we are judged more on our looks than on our abilities. Anger signals that something is wrong, and unacknowledged or unresolved anger can destroy anyone's ability to be mindful. So that this situation does not put us in further harm (we are already in harm's way due to whatever or whomever has made us angry or hurt) let us look to the following affirmations:

Mars, god of rage, set right the injustice that has distracted me from my mission.

One of the origin myths of the Hindu goddess Kali states that she is made up of all the rage that the other gods in their infinite love and goodness could not acknowledge or utilize. She therefore becomes the avenger, the one who can act when the other gods are impotent to do so.

Kali, take up my cause and fight where I cannot.

Remember that there is nothing wrong with "giving it all to God/dess." Sometimes it's the only way to get through the day.

Whatever you want to call it—mindfulness, being on-task, being here now, and so on—if you pay attention to what you are doing in the here and now you will go a long way toward letting the gods into your life more effectively and being happier, more centered, and more fulfilled in your daily life. Consider my example:

The Accident

I had many things on my mind. Various recent misfortunes were among them, but also this book, the Iseum's upcoming Beltaine ritual, and the fact that I'd somehow gotten lost going to my co-priestess' (Lori Nyx) apartment, a place I've visited probably a thousand times before. Now, I'm not one of those directionally challenged people. In fact, normally I'm the one who finds the way when everyone else is lost.

I should have known that my mind was elsewhere when I took that wrong turn. I'm still a bit too young to be having a "senior moment," so I should have known right there that my mind was elsewhere and that I needed to be more mindful. Unfortunately, at the time that my mind was elsewhere, my foot was on the gas pedal.

I stopped at the stop sign, let a car go by, and then accelerated to cross the street. What I didn't notice was the OTHER car coming my way. He hit the brakes but it was too late; because he was driving a 1969 Ford, made of steel, and I was driving a 2002 Chevy, made of plastic, my car made it across the street but its bumper did not. His car had nary a scratch that I could see, but the rear bumper of my car was lying in the road several yards away from my vehicle. And, of course, because I had the stop sign, I was at fault for the accident.

A $500 deductible is a lot to spend just to learn mindfulness.

So now let's review mindfulness and what it means.

To be mindful is to be "in the moment." Right here, right now, there is nothing going on but what IS. What IS is ALL there IS. Let's make it a mantra:

What IS
Is ALL
There IS.
Right here,
Right now,
What IS
Is ALL
There IS.

Repeat as necessary until you believe it.

We always seem to be running off somewhere doing something else other than what we're supposed to be doing and then complaining about how much we have to do. Our endlessly "connected" society is actually more disconnected than ever. For example, I saw two women having lunch, and one of them was talking on her cell phone. I wanted to go up and ask her, "So, when you have lunch with Maria do you talk on the phone with Marcy, and when you have lunch with Marcy do you talk on the phone with Maria?" I think I'll try that one someday and see what happens.

In order to re-connect with the real world we need to be here now. The person we are with RIGHT NOW is real and is here; the person on the other end of the telephone or computer modem is NOT here RIGHT NOW and so is "less real" than your immediate companion. Mindfulness, remember, also means prioritizing. If you have a job where you work with both customers in person and on the phone, remember that the customer who is in person should get priority, unless he or she walked up while you were already on the phone. Everyone wants to be treated as if he or she were special; the only way to do that is to acknowledge and respect that person sitting or standing in front of you. For the moment, in the here and now, he or she is your world.

It's not just manners or a sense of appropriate priorities that I'm talking about. Mindfulness can help you from becoming a crime statistic. Be alert to who or what is around you; keep your valuables safe; don't flash large bills or expensive jewelry in a crowd; and, when walking to your car, take a good look around to make sure no one is lying in wait for you. These are dangerous times we live in. Visualize your "shield" whenever you think you need it most (see Chapter 7). Walking out of the mall at night near Christmas with your arms full of packages is one such example.

Use your built-in radar to keep yourself safe. We usually know when someone is behind us even if we don't see or hear him or her, and when someone is staring at us we feel it and look around. Rely on your senses, including that sixth sense. Even police officers will tell you to trust your instincts and intuition; we have not lost all of our animal senses and can still anticipate danger if we just pay attention to our surroundings and are tuned in to our senses.

This might mean that sometimes feeling is more important than thinking. Many a bad situation has happened because the person ignored his or her sense of impending danger and thought "it was all in my head."

Sensing the kind of energy that is present in a situation is a marvelous indicator of what's really going on or is about to go on. If you can sit or stand quietly and just allow yourself to *feel* the tenor of the situation, you can usually guess correctly about the atmosphere and act accordingly. For example, are those kids in baggy clothing over there just roughhousing and kidding around with each other, or is a gang fight about to break out? People have gotten caught in the crossfire because they didn't pay attention to their feelings, and others have jumped to the wrong conclusions—sometimes also with disastrous results—when the situation was completely harmless.

So how does all of this affect the practice of magick, and the spirituality of our kind? Simple: In order to perform magick, the first requirement is the ability to *focus* on the task at hand! Nowadays with half the kids on the block on Ritalin and people being diagnosed all over the place with Adult Attention Deficit Disorder, it is clear that there is something very wrong with our society. We need to begin counteracting it and to learn mindfulness in the service of the gods and in the practice of magick.

In other words, it is not for no reason that the people who generally are thought of when we talk about meditation or "stillness" are people in religious orders. No, they're not "contemplating their navels" as some unenlightened folks want to believe. To contemplate nothingness is also to be aware of the great One that is All there is. If you've ever meditated, you know what I mean. If you haven't, well, there's no time better than the present to get started!

In stillness we not only can contemplate the beauty of nature but also the form and function of the universe, which is, in its own way, beautiful—just ask a cosmologist! In focusing out mental energy we can do amazing things. In many ways, the first step toward being a successful practitioner of magick is the learning of mindfulness.

In mindfulness we not only do the gods' work but we also quiet ourselves enough to hear "that still small voice within," which may well be the voice of Deity. What is it saying? We have to be still in order to truly hear it.

The real test of mindfulness is, of course, to be able to quiet yourself and stay on-task in the middle of all the anarchy that passes for modern life. It would be great if we could all go on retreats and be in a quiet, beautiful place in order to experience mindfulness. Well, duh, it's easy then! Why do you think those monks shut themselves up in monasteries? No outside distractions for them! Sometimes I envy them….

Nevertheless, most of us live in noisy cities or suburbs and rarely get the peace and quiet we really need. That's why they invented white noise machines, you see! Trying to find true peace and quiet can be a daunting task at times. However, mindfulness does not require it. It only requires that we focus on one thing at a time—that is, tune out the other distractions. Watch a machinist sometime. He probably has the noisiest job on the block and yet look at how he concentrates while doing his job. He has to, or some of his body parts could end up being ground round in those machines! But he is able to focus and therefore be successful in his job, no matter how noisy it is.

Ideally, your living quarters should provide you with at least some quiet time. Everyone needs a quiet place to relax and regroup. If you do not have this space at home, you may have to seek it out elsewhere. Then you can gather your thoughts and focus when you need to, but also relax when you need to. You can't have one without the other. And that's why the machinist goes to happy hour after work!

Practice mindfulness with the following spell:

The Mindfulness Over Matter Spell

This spell is done at home regardless of what else is going on. Keep the phone turned on. Let the guys watch the game. Let the tots eat the Play-Doh or continue whatever mischief they're up to. Hopefully the landscapers will have their leaf-blowers on full bore. The more distractions, the better.

Set up your altar in the usual way. Cast a circle. Now sit before the altar and pick up, one at a time, each of the various objects you would normally keep on your altar. Touch, caress, smell, listen to, or even taste (if appropriate) each item. Can you keep your concentration on that item when everything else around you is bedlam? Of course not. But that doesn't mean you shouldn't try.

There's something called the Crying Child Syndrome. It's a situation where you're trying to give a speech, watch a film, do a ritual, and so forth, but somewhere a child is crying. This is the universe saying, "Hello! Remember me? You must have been crazy to think I wouldn't pay attention to the fact that you're trying to hold the attention of all those other people. Get real! Life is what happens when you're trying to perform for others."

Now try the spell again when it's more quiet. See how well you can keep your mind on each altar object before your thoughts start to drift onto other things. Repeat this spell whenever you feel you are losing focus on your magick or your spirituality.

Chapter 4

Dialogues With Dieties: How to Talk to a God

Note: I am indebted to Lori Nyx and Francisco Arcaute for their comments and suggestions on these meditations. And, by the way, the Cosmos bar in L.A.'s Little Tokyo is a fine place to talk about the gods.

Affirmations

The Goddess hears my prayers.

ಸಿ

The Shining One hears my prayers.

ಸಿ

The gods hear my prayers.

❦

My prayers are answered.

For most of us, our first "dialogue" with deity took place in childhood, when we were taught to kneel, hold our hands in "prayer" position, and recite such lines as, "If I die before I wake, I pray the Lord my soul to take." Yikes! Scary stuff for young children! And they wonder why we grow up fearful and twisted. Needless to say, many of us don't really know how to *talk with* a deity, and many of us are even sort of frightened by the idea.

In coming to paganism from the Abrahamic beliefs (defined as Judaism, Christianity, and Islam) we may wonder if what we are really doing is "idol worship" or some other idea we have gotten from our religious heritage. Well, that's actually not completely incorrect. After all, in ancient Egypt, it was believed that during a ritual the gods really did come down and possess their statues. In modern sects such Voudou, Santeria, and Candomble, the deities are believed to possess their followers.

However, most of us know that we are not "praying to idols" but merely utilizing statues or pictures as a focal point, a symbol of our devotion. We need to make sure we have cast off worn out assumptions about our relationship with deity before we attempt to work with these energies in any major way. Simply put, we need to lighten up!

I was told that my grandfather once made a joke that offended his mother-in-law, who called the joke blasphemous. He told her that he meant it as humor, not blasphemy, for he believed that "God knows when I'm kidding." In other words, he trusted God to understand his meaning as humor and not as disrespect; he was practicing what Lori Nyx calls "reverent irreverence."

Humor, in fact, has a hugely important place in our worship. In fact, some of our deities make sure the joke's on us, at least some of the time! This kind of informal discourse with the deities is immensely important in feeling the immanence of the gods that is essential to the understanding of our path and is one of the most rewarding aspects of it.

The simplest way to approach a deity is just to say, "Lady (or Lord), please hear me. I've been having a really tough time lately." Then go on with your story. Our gods understand that we sometimes need to get things off our chests, and when there's no one else to talk to, the gods are always there to listen. That in itself should give one a feeling of enormous relief and an island of peace in the eye of the hurricane.

What about all that bended-knee stuff, hand gestures, lighting candles, praying before statues or pictures, and so forth? That is all very well and good if you wish to do it. Some traditions, in fact, demand it. An example is the way one prays to Shiva in the Hindu manner. (See Chapter 6.) In another example, when approaching Yemaya at the shore, you should walk sideways into the water because approaching her (the sea) face-first is considered by practitioners of Santeria to be disrespectful.

But many pagan traditions do not call for these actions, especially if the "dialogue" takes place outside of a formal circle or ritual. To speak to a god or goddess in everyday life is to speak to a friend.

As I said, this is hard for a lot of people, even those who weren't raised in the one of the three Abrahamic religions. So if you want to practice Lori Nyx's reverent irreverence, it helps to regard the gods as "people," as she is fond of calling them. The examples that follow are just that; this is certainly not a comprehensive list of deities, but rather a soupcon of examples.

If you wish to ascribe to this path, read the descriptions here and address the appropriate deity as you would an actual person. Let's face it, however: Some deities are forces of nature that we know little about. You may not feel comfortable calling a particular god "Dude" even though some of them obviously fit the bill. Some others, however, have a long intellectual history that fits the modern sensibility well. It all depends on with whom you work. I have (quite irreverently, but sincerely) dubbed a variety of approachable deities into categories that we as modern people can understand, and I have used modern archetypes such as celebrities and fictional characters as a contemporary way of thinking of them. If nothing else, you might get a kick out of imagining the deities this way.

When one works with a deity for a long period of time, he or she becomes as comfortable as an old shoe. For example, I am a Priestess of Thoth, and one of my statues of Thoth has a head that looks less like the ibis it is supposed to be and somewhat more like a turkey vulture; fortunately, my long-standing relationship with this *neter* allows me to be comfortable calling him "Ol' Turkey Neck" just in passing. But of course, in a formal ritual I would never do so!

Comfort, however, is a marvelous thing—but it usually has to be earned. You gotta break those new shoes in first. So work with me on this one.

Okay, here we go:

CEOs/Generals

These are the boss gods, those who metaphorically head the corporation-like structures of religious pantheons. They are to be approached as such; therefore, you would speak to them in the most formal manner of any of the gods. Although due to the television series *The Adventures of Hercules,* I will always think of the late Anthony Quinn as Zeus, I can also imagine a Donald Trump-like Zeus saying, "YOU'RE FIRED!" and his consort Hera resembling Martha Stewart as she torments one of Zeus's mistresses. Boss gods may also be imagined as generals of armies or navies. Approach these deities with respect and deference. On the other hand, I can also somewhat imagine Richard Branson as a more laid-back CEO/Deity, maybe Danu.

Deities: Brahma, Damballah, Danu, Demeter, Durga, Hades, Hera, Juno, Jupiter, Mars, Morrigan, Mut, Neith, Odin, Ogun, Oldumare, Olorun, Perun, Poseidon, Sekhmet, Zeus.

Teachers/Mentors

These are the gods who teach us and guide us in our professions, our lives, our arts. Think of Sidney Poitier in *To Sir, With Love,* Julie Andrews in *The Sound of Music,* or librarian/mentor Giles in *Buffy the Vampire Slayer* when you think of these wise, patient entities. These are also the mother and father gods. Though they are to be given the respect of an authority figure, they are also your friends, and repeated interaction with them can certainly initiate one into the joys of a more intimate relationship with these deities. After all, mentors and teachers expect you to question and challenge them from time to time as proof of continued critical thinking, learning, and growing.

Deities: Apollo, Artemis, Athena, Brigit, Bragi, Diana, Flora, Hermes, Isis, Kwan Yin, Lugh, Mokosh, Osiris, Oya, Poseidon, Sarasvati, Shu, Tefnut, Thoth, Vishnu.

Professors Emeriti/Boards of Directors

The wise professor who has retired and the board member who can corral the CEO when he gets out of line fit into this category. For example, imagine the old shareholders being summoned—presumably from Mount Olympus—to deal with a CEO who doesn't particularly want to clean out his desk (a giant corporation built on cute rodents is a recent example that comes to mind). If I ever made a movie about the Egyptian gods I'd cast Abe Vigoda as the senescent Ra. I'd also cast Gloria Stuart as Hecate. You get the idea. These are also the grandmother and grandfather gods. They can be a bit cranky at times, as are all old ones, but their wisdom has no bounds. Remember this joke: Why do grandparents and grandkids get along so well? Because they have a common enemy.

Deities: Amun, Baba Yaga, Babalu-Aye, Eleggua, Hecate, Kali, Mut, Neptune, Olodumare, Old Woman (Native American deity), Olorun, Papa Legba, Ra, Skadi, Spider Grandmother.

Dudes

These are your buds, and with whom you may drink or smoke. Ahem. They are the playful nature deities who don't take things as seriously nor are as formal as the deities in the previous categories. The archetypal Dude, of course, is Jeff Bridges in *The Big Lebowski*; or you can think of any other buddy movie you may have seen, such as those made by Bob Hope and Bing Crosby or any movie where two guys team up—for example, Eddie Murphy and Nick Nolte, or Jackie Chan and Chris Tucker. These are also gods of such "mortal" issues as sex and death. You may speak to them the way you'd speak to any of your good friends.

Deities: Anansi, Anubis, Balder, Cernunnos, Chango, Coyote, Dionysus, Hapi, Herne, Horus, Khonsu, Loki, Lugh, Ochosi, Pan, Ptah, Shiva, Sucellos, Thor, Volos.

Girlfriends

Girlfriends are the female equivalents of Dudes (known here in the "land of the Beach Boys" as *Dude-ettes*). Think of the four friends in *Waiting to Exhale*; wasn't Angela Bassett the very wrath of the goddess when she torched her ex's car? What about the women on *Sex in the City*? *Thelma and Louise* are Valkyries by other names. Like the the Dudes, these gals often are about sex and death, so watch whom you rag on when you talk to them. Treat them as girlfriends and they'll treat you the same way.

Deities: Aphrodite, Bastet, Brigit, Freya, Hathor, Lakshmi, Nantosuelta, Oshun, Parvati, Persephone, Rhiannon, Rusalka, Sati, Venus, Yemaya.

☙

Here are some ideas for offerings to give the deities if you keep an altar to any one or more of them. For a simpler altar set-up, see Chapter 7.

Asian/Pacific Gods: Peaches, oranges, grapefruit, tangerines; tea (the real thing, not herbal), plum wine, sake; cooked rice, lotus cakes.

African/Afro-Caribbean Gods (orishas, loas): Pumpkin, coconut, watermelon; rum, cachaca (cane liquor), anisette or Opal Nera; cooked chicken or duck, yams, honey, candies, tobacco.

Egyptian/Middle Eastern Gods (neteru): Dates, raisins, figs, pomegranates; beer, wine, mead; couscous, lamb, pita bread, matzo crackers, baklava, lotus cakes.

Greek/Roman Gods: Olives, pomegranates, grapes; red wine, retsina, anisette; saffron rice, olive oil, pita bread, eggplant, fish.

Norse/Celtic/Slavic Gods: Apples, berries, plums; mead, beer, vodka, aquavit; pork, salmon, oatcakes, rye bread, hard-boiled eggs, caviar.

Hindu/Tibetan Gods: Oranges, bananas, mangoes; milk, tea; nuts, honey, candies, Indian sweets, lotus cakes, hemp.

Native American/Mesoamerican Gods: Cranberries, wild berries (bearberries, huckleberries, and so on), mangoes, papayas, coconuts; rum, tequila, herbal teas; cooked game, chicken, fry bread, candies, tobacco.

When in doubt, visit an ethnic market. You may have to cross cultures a bit; for example, you can buy lotus cakes in a Chinese bakery, and they make equally nice offerings for East Asian, Egyptian, and Hindu deities. Many traditional offerings are available nowadays that in the past required substitutions; for example, tisanes (herb teas) from around the world as well as the herbal teas the Native Americans use are available commercially now, and those of us in the United States no longer have to substitute rum for the cane liquor called for in some Afro/Latin rituals. Cachaca is now available in better-stocked liquor departments, such as those in Bristol Farms.

But what do we want to do when we wish to contact a deity in a somewhat more formal manner? Guided visualization is become more and more prevalent in the pagan/Wiccan community. Here are three guided visualizations for you to try when needed. These are fairly advanced, and if you haven't done much meditation or visualization you'll want to become familiar with it first before trying these.

In addition, after these three you will find a "do-it-yourself" template for writing your own guided visualizations.

Guided Visualizations

A more intense way to contact Deity is through guided visualization. Here are some guided meditations for you to try based on my ideas of how to approach deities. Read them carefully before attempting to follow them. Record them yourself or, better yet, have a friend read them to you with a background of soft music, as a lot of people feel "safer" attempting an inner-plane journey with a friend nearby. After you've tried the appropriate examples, create your own visualizations using the "do-it-yourself" suggestions that follow.

You will always be asked to drink something—symbolically, of course—during the meditation. There is a very good reason for this. It helps to ground you, and is much easier to visualize than trying to pretend to eat something during the meditation. So follow the guidelines in the meditations even if they call for you to drink something that you wouldn't normally drink. After the meditation, ground yourself more literally by having a light snack and drinking something non-alcoholic.

The three meditations are listed in increasing order of formality. The meditation to Damballah is the most serious one on this list, so I will start with the lighter ones first.

I hope you will have fun with these and then will be creative and try to write some of your own.

Goin' to the Roadhouse: Thor

We begin with one of our Dudes: Thor. Known for his big hammer and his red braids, Thor is not only a mighty warrior who might lend a hand if you need a leg up, to coin a phrase, but is also often the butt of jokes in the Norse pantheon! In one story, for example, his hammer is stolen and he has to disguise himself as a woman in order to get it back. If you need him you'll find him in the mead hall. He is probably the most Dude-like of any of the Dudes I've listed.

(This meditation is dedicated to the memory of my cousin, James Hicks.)

Imagine yourself on a long, straight, dusty highway. What are you driving? Visualize your vehicle now.

You feel the road beneath you, smell the various scents of the trip, be they hay and grass, farm animals, or dust. This is no urban freeway. You feel a great sense of freedom and solitude driving up this road. Take your time and enjoy the journey.

It's been a long drive up Route 66, and you see a building up ahead. It's hot and dusty but the trip has been worth it, because now you approach the entrance to the infamous Bagdad Cafe in Newbury Springs, California. Here you'll meet probably one of the most interesting and most oddly lovable characters in Norse mythology, the Aesir God Thor.

Open the screen door and enter the café. Turn left to enter the bar. Then sit down at the bar, and ask for cold beer. "Make that a pitcher," says a figure who has suddenly appeared on your left. You turn your head and find yourself seated next to a large, imposing man. He is not blond the way the Marvel comic book character is, but rather his hair is braided into two red braids not unlike those of Willie Nelson. Does he resemble Willie Nelson to you? Or, does he look to you like any number of character actors who have portrayed bikers in any number of films or any persons you may have known in your real life who remind you of one? Even Jim Morrison may for you have a certain resemblance to Thor, for the roadhouse is certainly his element.

Although Thor does appear to have a beer belly, he also has very muscular arms and huge shoulders. He does not wear a hat with Viking horns, however. Instead, he wears no head-covering whatsoever and you see that next to him on the bar are actually a motorcycle helmet and the pair of sunglasses. You turn to greet him and he greets you in turn with a hearty handshake, then puts his arm around you and gives you a bone-crushing hug. Clearly, Thor is a much more welcoming deity than you may have expected.

The waitress brings a pitcher of beer and two mugs. Thor insists on pouring it. He pours you each a large mug of the frothy beer then insists that you make the toast and asks, "To whom would you like us to toast?"

And you're understandably nervous and you don't know what to say.

Thor proposes a toast. "To the ancestors," he says.

"To the ancestors," you reply. You two clink your glasses together and he smiles and says, "What brings you here today, buddy? What can I do for you?"

What would be appropriate to speak or ask about? Think about it. For example, let's say you would like to buy a motorcycle, but you don't know how your family, friends, spouse, or co-workers would react. If you ask Thor about this, he is sure to laugh! Listen to what he says as a reply and think about what you really want to do. Thor is about nothing if he is not about individuality and being who you want to be. But he also explains that with individuality comes responsibility, and if you are not ready to take on that responsibility, then perhaps you're not ready to take on anything that would make you feel uncomfortable in the presence of others.

"Let's hear some tunes!" he says. He goes over to the jukebox and looks at the selections. What selections would Thor choose? Think about this for moment, and when you do this meditation you may want those tunes in the background to help you increase the feeling that you are actually there in the Bagdad Cafe with Thor. You may also wish to have a glass of beer next to where you are doing this meditation. This meditation is better worked with while sitting up than while lying down.

Thor senses that you have some issues with personal liberty. He also senses that you would like more of a sense of freedom in your life. He tells you that, though it is true that others can make you un-free, it is only yourself who can make you free.

Now discuss anything else you wish to with Thor. If this is all you have to say to him today, finish your beer. You may wish to shake his hand, but he will probably prefer to clap you on the back and hug you with one of his bone-crushing embraces again. Do not be frightened if at any time during this meditation you feel the physical presence of Thor even to the point where you feel as though someone has actually patted you on the back or put a hand on your shoulder. The Norse Gods manifest physically rather than aurally or visually like gods from other pantheons. If you feel the sensation during the meditation be assured that it is simply means that you are in the presence of the Norse Deities. You are in no danger. After all, who better than Thor to protect you during a meditation?

When you and Thor are finished with your chat, thank him. Tell him that you will raise a toast to him at your very next opportunity. Have you promised anything to Thor? If so, then he may ask you to swear an oath. The swearing of oaths was very, very important in the Norse pantheon and it simply means that you are giving your word to do what you say you are going to do. If he asks you to swear an oath, raise your glass, toast, and then say what ever else he asks you to say. If you do not feel comfortable with anything that he tells you to do, you may politely decline. If he has asked you to say anything particularly strange and you decline to do so, however, he may burst out laughing and you may realize that indeed his trickster friend Loki has come along for the ride. Only Loki would ask you to swear to something ridiculous or inappropriate.

It may seem strange that someone such as Loki would be best friends with Thor. However, the trickster aspect of Loki fits in very well with the informal demeanor of Thor. If Loki seems to intrude on your meeting with Thor, you may always take him aside and tell him that you are uncomfortable with Loki. However, Thor will probably say that Loki is no problem and that he can handle the situation if anything goes awry.

You may wish to stay in the Bagdad Cafe for awhile with Thor and anyone else who happens to wander in. If you stay there you may find yourself in the company of a variety of deities from the Norse and other pantheons. Sometimes, it is fun to just observe and imagine what these deities would be like if they were actually there socializing with each other and with you. When you're ready to go, make sure you leave a large tip! Thor would certainly not want to seem cheap in front of his friends, and you of course are one of his friends, so he will leave an even bigger tip.

You need do nothing else except say goodbye to leave the Bagdad Cafe, and get into your car or, you may find that your car has transformed into a beautiful new motorcycle. Perhaps it is a Harley-Davidson, perhaps another type of motorcycle that you have been particularly interested in. If this is the case, return to your waking consciousness after you have returned down Route 66 to your home. Take your time. Do not worry if you don't live anywhere that has access to Route 66; just visualize this mythical highway in your mind. If you wish to know what the Bagdad Cafe is like and you can't make it to Newberry Springs, California, read the Website. I think you'll find it interesting.

To get into the spirit of the Norse Gods, it would be nice to burn some birch or pine incense, or better yet to get some woodsy essential oils and put them in your diffuser. Keep some beer or mead in the refrigerator, and toast the Norse Gods when you have a drink. If you want to make a more concrete offering to Thor (for example, if you are a motorcycle enthusiast you can find some information on the Internet about groups that might aid in, for example, medical bills for bikers who have been injured); certainly this would be a charity Thor would appreciate you giving to as an offering. Many motorcycle clubs also collect toys for children at Christmas, and this too would be a highly approved-of charity.

Whenever you feel the need to speak with Thor again, and I would suggest that should do so on a Thursday or Friday night, you may do this meditation again. Wednesday or Tuesday night would also be appropriate. I think you will find Thor an amiable companion, and one who will occasionally test you.

Interestingly enough, if you do this meditation often enough, you may not even have to have essential oils in a diffuser. Why not? Because when you do this meditation after having done so a few times, you may find that the scent of the forest comes to you automatically. (Or perhaps the scent of beer. Trickster gods, remember?)

If you work with the Norse Gods on a regular basis I would suggest getting a Thor's hammer to wear as an amulet while doing this meditation or doing any other sorts of workings with them. If you really want to toast them in a special way in the "real" world, look for a beautiful bottle of Thor's Hammer Vodka, a premium vodka that is well worth the cost. Sip slowly and think of the ice of Iceland and the volcanoes as well. Fire and ice, ice and fire.

This is what the Norse Deities are all about.

Tender Mercies: Kwan Yin

Kwan Yin, known throughout Asia, is the goddess of compassion, mercy, and understanding. Even when the indigenous polytheistic religions of Asia fell to Buddhism and Confucianism, Kwan Yin, the most loving, most compassionate mother, remained, even in the most patriarchal societies. She is the very embodiment of empathy, the patient mother who accepts all, understands all, forgives all.

There are many versions of the Kwan Yin story; one told by Buddhists goes as follows. Avalokiteshvara (also known as Kwannon; the Japanese still use the name Kwannon for the goddess) was a bodhisattva who wished to know true compassion and mercy, but felt he could not do so fully while trapped in the body of a male, considering all their warlike, hierarchical tendencies. So he had himself turned into a woman: Kwan Yin. Even once Kwan Yin learned perfect compassion, pity, and empathy, she vowed to stay on Earth—as opposed to going on to Nirvana—as long as there was a need for compassion in the world. And so she is still with us now.

We all need a little mercy and compassion, peace, and quiet in this hustling, bustling world. In this meditation, you will enter an archetypal busy cityscape, and then escape to Kwan Yin's garden of peace and serenity. All of us need this meditation from time to time, as stress is one of the most pervasive ills of our society.

Imagine that you are in a downtown area of a large city. If you have been to Los Angeles's Chinatown and Saigon Plaza on which this scene was modeled, imagine that. If not, then imagine the Chinatown area of, say, New York, Vancouver, San Francisco, or any large city.

Outside the buildings are gray; the sidewalks are gray; the air is gray. Cars dash about, spewing pollutants into the air. People rush by you on all sides, carrying packages, barking into cell phones, or, some of them, rifling through trash cans trying to find a bite to eat.

You look up and see a crowded freeway, and you wonder where everyone is dashing off to so quickly. Does all the hurrying around seem to you to have a purpose? Why is everything so gray and grim? Heat rises from the pavement, and many unpleasant smells: garbage, urine, even fear.

Just as you begin to feel the oppressiveness of the city you notice across the street a bright neon sign advertising an indoor shopping center. What does the neon sign say? Meditate on this for a moment.

You decide to enter the shopping complex. Once inside, the air is fresh and cool. If any place could be the opposite of what you've experienced outside, this place is it. In place of the gray wasteland is a riot of color. Brightly colored silk *cheongsams* and other lovely and exotic clothing are for sale. Vendors sell gold, silver, and jade jewelry, and a variety of sparkling gemstones. Still other vendors have decorative lamps in neon and blinking colored lights.

The noise here is different, but still overwhelming: salespeople talking, music blaring, wind-up toys squawking, cash registers ringing, and all the sounds of commerce going on all at once. Although this is a much happier place than the one outside, it is also paced at a fever pitch, and you soon realize that you have exchanged one frenetic pace for another. Though the scents here are by comparison far more pleasant than those outdoors, you begin to realize that what smells like flowers are cheap, synthetic fragrances, and those mouth-watering cooking smells are just those of greasy fast food.

You feel that you're the filling in a city sandwich, stuck between two sides of the urban nightmare. Yet you sense that there is something here that you have missed so far, and that if you can just find it, you may find a sanctuary and learn the way to cope with the pace of modern life.

You walk into a shop with brightly lit lamps and colorful statuary. Your senses are dazzled by all the colors and shapes until your eyes alight on one item: a sculpture of a beautiful, mature Asian lady seated on a large pink lotus blossom, her hands appearing to give a benediction. This is a statue of Kwan Yin, and though it looks to be fragile porcelain, you are sure it is much stronger than it appears.

Keep looking at the statue. Focus on the shape of Kwan Yin's face, the drape of her robes, the blushing petals of the lotus. All around you begins to blur as you focus solely on this image. Soon the electric lamps vanish, and the light that shines is from the sun.

The artificial flowers, plastic gewgaws, and electronic noises give way to lovely gingko trees, weeping willows, chrysanthemums, and peonies. The music becomes very simple: It may be merely the songs of birds, or the single notes of Japanese or Chinese classical music. The strong chemical scents of the cologne give way to the fresh scents of green plants, flower petals, and freshly turned earth. Take a deep breath now, and close your eyes. Count down now from 10 to one: ten, nine, eight, seven, six, five, four, three, two, and one. Now with your real eyes still closed, open your eyes in the visualization. You see before you Kwan Yin, but she is human now and very much alive, and you stand face to face. Her robes are softly shimmering colors of pale green, yellow, and pink. Her face is plump and kindly, the face of a mature, very wise, and beautiful woman. A sort of Mona Lisa smile is on her face, mysterious and a bit mischievous.

In front of her is a traditional tea set. You can smell the steam from the tea. She bows to you and asks you if you will partake of tea with her. You bow to her, more deeply than she has bowed to you in order to show respect, and say yes. She pours a cup for you and then for herself, and indicates that you are to drink first.

Taste the tea. It is a light brown color, not as light as green tea nor as dark as black tea. This is Ti Quan Yin, a specific type of Chinese tea dedicated to the goddess. It is sold in Asian tea shops everywhere and you realize that when you leave this place you may go to one of those shops and buy some of it to take home with you.

Sip the tea and feel its warmth suffusing your body. Feel your tension melt away, and, with it, your stress and pessimism. Be aware of your posture. Are you kneeling, sitting on your heels? This is one traditional meditation posture and you might try it for this meditation, or else use the cross-legged meditation posture most of us are familiar with.

Kwan Yin faces you, also kneeling, and you are eye to eye with her. Her dark glossy hair is done up in a kind of bun; does she remind you of anyone? A mother or grandmother figure, a trusted friend? Have you seen echoes of her face in teachers, nurses, therapists, librarians, or in artists, writers, or performers? Perhaps you tell Kwan Yin that you saw actress Bai Ling portray her in the TV movie. Kwan Yin will laugh and say she is flattered by the portrayal. After this meditation, search for a touch of Kwan Yin's demeanor in women you know and especially in any new women you may meet after this meditation (and men, for don't forget that Kwan Yin was once a man.)

You may stay and enjoy your tea and any ceremonial gestures that Kwan Yin may do—this may be different for each person who does the meditation, and different each time one repeats it. Does she offer you anything? Does she ask you if you have anything in particular you'd like to ask her?

Feel free to pour out your heart to Kwan Yin. Tell her where you need rest, respite, surcease from sorrow in your life. Cry if you need to. Kwan Yin's understanding smile and kind eyes speak louder than words. You know that at any time you are welcome to visit her garden, and feel the blessings of a calm, serene oasis in the midst of all the hustle and bustle. She may even ask you to lie down for a while on her tatami mats and silk pillows, gazing up at the lush greenery and the birds and other charming creatures that live amongst the trees. Smell the jasmine and cherry blossoms. Feel the balmy yet refreshing breeze, and listen to the babbling brook and the sighing branches of the willow tree.

When you are ready to go, bow deeply to Kwan Yin. Thank her for your opportunity to repose in her sanctuary. Now each of you stands, and you turn and see rice paper screens sectioning off this space. She pulls back the screens, and you are ready to return to the life outside. But wait. Is there something she wants to tell you? Something she wants to give you before you leave? If so, take it. If she has a task for you to do, such as plant a lily bulb or hang a bagua mirror on your front door, make sure you do it after the meditation is over.

Now take three deep pranic breaths, and step out of her sanctuary. Take one more breath, and when you turn around, you see the garden you were in is gone, and there is simply the porcelain statue on a shelf, smiling knowingly at you.

Statues of Kwan Yin abound in Asian gift stores; you can find small, very budget-friendly ones, life-size bronze extremely expensive sculptures, and everything in between. Get yourself a Kwan Yin statue, and a box of Ti Quan Yin tea. You might also like to get a small crystal candle holder in the shape of a lotus and burn a candle for her, offer a cup of her tea and bow to her altar. Burn jasmine, rose, or orange blossom incense.

Visit Kwan Yin whenever you need to. Do not skip the cityscape features of the meditation, however; Kwan Yin wants you to see how hard life really is so that you may become more compassionate as well. Only by going through such trials can one truly understand the nature of mercy.

Have mercy for yourself and others! Buy yourself some nice soothing Asian meditation music. Indian chants do well here also. I like the recording of Shiva praise songs called *Jiva Mukti*. Many of the recordings of Deva Premal contain songs that are chants to the Hindu gods; some of her songs also celebrate the Orishas.

Make a child laugh today. This would cheer Kwan Yin more than giving your whole paycheck to a charity. Bite your tongue and listen when your best friend has a problem, even when you've just had a lousy day and have a pounding headache. Hug a willow tree in the park.

With each journey of compassion that we take, we come a bit closer to the Bodhisattva consciousness of Kwan Yin.

How like a god/dess! Perhaps if enough people evince these traits Kwan Yin may in time find her role on earth no longer necessary and join the enlightened ones where she so richly deserves to be.

Though I suspect that each act of compassion she does is, somehow, far more satisfying than whatever one calls Enlightenment or Nirvana. But hey, that's just my way of looking at it.

Tell It on the Mountain: Damballah

Damballah is the creator deity of Haiti; he is the "serpent" part of the serpent and the rainbow (the rainbow being his consort, Ayida-Wedo). As a multi-colored serpent Damballah stretches across the sky, as his reflection Ayida-Wedo is the rainbow cast upon the water. The two of them together create all life from a world egg that is often shown being cradled between the two of them. As the supreme creator he is seen as the deity who can bestow the gift of creativity upon individuals, and he especially loves his children who dedicate themselves to creative pursuits. He is a powerful force and one to be approached with much care and respect. He dresses in white linen, as do deities from many different cultures, interestingly enough.

Robert Johnson, so the story goes, met the Devil at the crossroads and exchanged his soul for musical talent. Those within the Afro/Caribbean community would laugh at that version, however, saying that he merely met the loa Papa Legba there and paid him $3 (sometimes it's inflated to $7!) for the means toward a successful musical career. In this guided meditation, you will meet the vodou loa Damballah and receive his blessing and guidance on your chosen career path. I would especially recommend this meditation for those who wish to have a career connected to music, art, writing, acting, or any of the creative arts, but you can of course ask for other career paths of the loa.

And the best part is you don't have to sell your soul or write a check payable to "Papa Legba, Esq."

Damballah is a heavy-duty individual, and this meditation might be a bit frightening to some people. There are built-in safeguards during this meditation so that if you feel uncomfortable you can exit the visualization and try it again on a day when you feel more daring.

Imagine yourself in a Haitian village near the mountains. It is obvious to you that the people there are poor monetarily but are spiritually rich. Their small homes are brightly painted and colorfully decorated with artwork made from old tin advertising signs, sacred decorations called *veves,* and the like. It is humid and warm, and the feeling of the tropics brings warmth to your bones.

The villagers are smiling at you as they go about their tasks, and they seem to know why you are here. Soon you feel someone tugging at your sleeve. You look down and see a little girl handing you a stick of sugar cane. You take it from her and try to offer her a coin, but she shakes her head and says in Creole that it is a gift.

A woman comes out of a house and asks if you would like some coffee before going on your trip. She says the trip will be arduous and you will need the energy. She tells you that the coffee was grown on the mountain where you are headed, and the strength of the mountain is within it. You tell her you would like the coffee and she nods. She disappears into a small house and soon returns with a china cup with fleurs-de-lys on its rim. She tells you the cup is very old, and you must sip slowly and hold it carefully.

You sit down on a fallen log. She brings fresh milk from her cow for the coffee; you stir the coffee with the stick of sugarcane. Drink slowly, feeling its dark power filling you with strength and resolve.

Now you are almost ready to embark on your journey.

The village *houngan* comes out of his house. He is an old man who wears sunglasses with one lens broken out, and he leans on a cane. He tells you that you can stop any time on your journey to meet Damballah if you don't feel ready or feel too afraid to go on. He wishes you well and gives you his blessing, and you are off.

It is a hard, muddy trip uphill, but it is also beautiful with tropical flowers and lush vegetation. Take your time; climbing is hard and you'll want to stop and enjoy the scenery along the way. What plants and trees do you see? What animals? You may see snakes; don't be afraid, for they won't bother you.

When you reach the top of the hill you see a small hut to the left. It is painted red and it seems almost to throb with life. On it are the designs that are the veves for Damballah and his consort, Ayida Wedo, painted in black on the front of the house, and you know you are in the right place. You approach and knock on the door three times. A dusky, raspy voice from inside says, "Enter." You open the door and step into the darkened hut.

It is nearly pitch black inside the hut. The only source of light seems to come from cracks in the thatched roof. As your eyes adjust you notice some ambient light with no obvious source. Some of the light is red, and some of the light seems to be produced by an invisible black light. You hear something rustling slightly overhead and you look up to see a snake winding its way around the rafters. You may be frightened, but it is important not to allow your fears to get to you. Remember that any time during this meditation if you feel you cannot continue or feel frightened or uncomfortable in any way, you may stop, turn around, and go back down the hill. Remember that the villagers are always welcoming and will give you their own blessing.

You hear a rasping sound in the corner and you can see in the dim light that a figure is seated there. He leans forward on his chair and his face, arms, and body come out of the shadows. His thick, curly hair has been relaxed and hangs to his shoulders, his face is very, very dark, and, though it is hard to distinguish his features in this dim light, you can see that he somewhat resembles the late jazz master Miles Davis. He wears a white linen shirt and pants, and when he leans forward you can hear the linen rustle against his skin almost as if it's the skin of a snake sloughing off. You realize then that you are truly in the presence of Damballah.

He asks you why you have come and you tell him that you need his advice. He smiles, but the smile is a bit unnerving. You ask him if you may petition him for some advice. He considers this for a minute, and then he says in a very deep voice, "Yes."

Give yourself plenty of time now when you record this meditation or have it read to you so that you can think about how you will speak to Damballah and what advice he will give you in return. Is he holding anything? If so, what does the object mean to you? Now Damballah rises from his chair and move sinuously, serpent-like. He takes a sack of cornmeal from another corner and begins to draw a *veve* in the middle of the room that will be a magickal symbol of value to your path. Make sure to make a good mental note of its shape and try to draw the symbol when the meditation is over.

When you're finished with his audience, bow to him. Damballah then tells you that he will want to know how you're doing and how well you have followed his advice. After all, if you ask advice of someone who is as important as Damballah, you must report back to him once you have taken some of his suggestions; he may be angry if he feels that you have not taken his advice or if you have not taken him seriously.

You bow again and then you leave. Closing the front door, you take one the last look back at the mysterious shack you just spent time in with Damballah. You can hardly imagine that you've actually spent time with the supreme deity of Vodou! And now you are ready, albeit on shaking legs, to hike back down the mountain. You walk slowly for fear of slipping and falling but, once you have made it down to the village, you know your trip has been successful. Some of the villagers come out to find out what has happened and, when you tell them that you had an audience with Damballah, some stop in their tracks and applaud. They can see by looking at you that you have had a successful audience, and you are ready to go take his advice, work hard, better your life, and achieve your dreams, especially if they relate to the creative arts.

You hear someone laugh and look around, seeing that the person laughing is the old houngan. You know now that the old houngan in the village is really Papa Legba, the opener of the way, and you wouldn't have gotten anywhere near Damballah without his approval! You offer your blessings to him and to the people of the village before you leave this meditation.

Once you have put into application Damballah's suggestions for your life, please bear in mind that you must now give something to him. One of the best ways to do this would be to give a donation to any Haitian relief agencies or any other charities that would benefit the people of Haiti or their relatives here in the United States. In addition, if you feel a kinship with Damballah's reptiles, you may want to instead give a donation to a reptile rescue organization or similar charity.

Damballah is an extremely powerful deity, and you probably will not be repeating this meditation on a regular basis; however, should you wish to have an audience with him again, in the future make sure that you make your offering to any of the charities I have just mentioned before you approach him for more advice.

And don't forget to report back to him with your progress! He'll be waiting to hear all about it.

How to Write Your Own Meditation

I want this book to be user-friendly, and so throughout I give the reader options for modifying and creating his or her own affirmations and prayers. What about guided meditations or visualizations, such as the previous ones? Wouldn't it be cool if you could write them yourself?

Well, there's no reason why you can't. Here is a template—along with a few words of advice—with which you can construct your own guided visualization. I will present it as a list of ingredients; you put it together and bake it your way! However, as with a cake, there are certain ingredients that can be modified, but a few that have to be there. These are the essential ingredients:

1. **Purpose.** Before you begin you should have a purpose in mind. *Why* do you want to contact a particular deity, spirit, or entity? Purpose or intent is the first thing you want to be clear about. Just a word of warning: If your purpose is "I want to meet Cthulhu in his house at R'lyeh just to see what he's like," uh, maybe that's not such a good idea. You should have a serious purpose, and though many deities have a sense of humor, they would not appreciate being contacted ceremonially for no good reason. Some better ideas:

- To connect with your patron deity.
- To experience the deities of your ancestors.
- To ask an earth-shaking question (NOT "Does Bobby like me?")
- To visit another realm.
- To hear a message a deity has been trying to communicate to you.
- To ask for healing.
- To ask for money. (Oh, no, wait—that's why you connect with DAD!)

2. **Deity.** Do you work with a particular god or goddess? If so, then this step is taken care of. If not, then think carefully about what deity you'd like to visualize. Do research before you start with one you haven't worked with before. In your research, be sure to learn about a particular deity or pantheon's milieu; as you may have noticed in the previous meditations, I placed my deities in situations where their presence made sense and would see that they (and you) were comfortable.

3. **Setting.** The context in which you meet your deity is important. Don't start a visualization before knowing where you're going to meet and what this place would look like. You will probably want to pick a

place—real or imagined—in which you feel safe, feel comfortable, and can easily visualize, perhaps a place you visit frequently or would like to visit. You may go to your "happy place" if you have one that you regularly visit during meditation or visualization, or you might want to do what I've done, and create other settings for your meditations. Believe it or not, this is the hardest part of the process! Some ideas:

Where is the locale you will visit? Is it:

1. Muir Woods, a primeval-looking forest?
2. A pink-sand beach on Bermuda?
3. The red rock country of Utah?
4. Joshua Tree National Monument, an alien-looking desert landscape?

What structures will you find there?

1. A Mongolian yurt?
2. A ruined British abbey?
3. An Egyptian temple?
4. A cave, mound, or burrow?

Who will you see there besides your deity?

1. Children playing on swing sets and other park equipment?
2. Villagers tending animals and working the fields?
3. Priests and priestesses performing a ritual?

> 4. Explorers and other intrepid types (Indiana Jones)?

4. **Time Limit.** Now that you have the big three out of the way, decide how long you want this meditation to be. Fifteen minutes? Half an hour? If it goes much longer than that you'll either get fidgety or fall asleep, I promise. So be realistic about how long you want to be in that other place. Leave plenty of pauses along the way when you record it in order to give yourself plenty of time to do and see what you wish to.

5. **Grounding.** Make sure you have something to ground yourself. To make the meditations earlier in this chapter perfectly safe, I added the grounding right into each meditation. Traditionally, however, you "ground" yourself *after* the meditation. If that's what you want to do, make sure you have something on hand after you do the visualization to ground yourself, such as crackers, bread, or cookies, and a grounding beverage, (NOT alcohol!). You might also want to have a pen and paper handy to record any words, ideas, or pictures that you experienced in the meditation.

6. **Context.** Now that you have your meditation set up, in what context will you use it? Will you read it to yourself on tape and then play the tape for yourself? Will you have the coven or circle over and have someone read it to all of you? Will it just be you and a close friend to read you the meditation? I suggest trying the final suggestion first. Then you'll know if

you will or won't feel comfortable doing the meditation alone. Once you have tried it a couple of times and are happy with it, then record it for yourself or present it to the group.

Most of all, have fun and be creative. This may be a challenge if you haven't done much writing before. But it doesn't take a great writer to think of a place, describe it in plain English, and then add the other elements. In time, the actions that are supposed to happen in a meditation will just come to you appropriately when you have decided on purpose, deity, and setting. Trust yourself and have fun!

There are other situations in which we may have to meet the gods on a not-so-wonderful occasion. What do you do when you're…

Mad at the Gods

I clearly remember a TV commercial for one of those Irish movies. The ad featured the late, great actor Richard Harris, and in the scene shown in the ad he was angrily beating on the surf with a stick. This image is what I think of when I think of being angry with the gods.

When, if ever, is it okay to be angry with the gods? Well, I won't presume to speak of any other culture's beliefs except that of our own Western culture. Oddly enough, many Western beliefs actually say it's okay to rant and rail at the gods when you feel they've let you down. I tend to agree with this belief. If anyone can take a full dose of my anger, it's gotta be a Deity. (Anyone else I let loose on would be reduced to cinders in a nanosecond!)

The gods love us even when we're angry; this is when we need their understanding the most and we need not fear reprisals. Let me give you an example:

Love on the Rocks, With a Twist

A romantic relationship was not going the way I wanted it to. In fact, I'd just been given the "it's not you; it's me," speech and the lukewarm "we can still be friends" nonsense. I wasn't having any part of it. I was mad at him, and I was mad at the gods.

I went home and took the small snow globe of Venus I'd bought at Caesar's Palace and which resided on the end table near the bed and threw it across the bedroom. On my Shiva altar I turned his picture to the wall and got rid of anything on his altar that alluded to him as a god of sexuality.

This is how things remained for about a week. Eventually I threw away the snow globe, and, though I had turned Shiva's picture back around, I left his altar bare of sexual aspects. Then in the middle of my snit, something more important took my attention away from my relationships with both the guy who dumped me and the deities who had formerly been my "love gods."

Someone I'd known for almost 20 years was dying. Only a few years older than myself, he was too young to die. He'd worked and done his other activities up until almost the very end; those of us who loved him were prepared to tell others that "he died with his boots on."

Though it wasn't unexpected, one is never prepared for death, not really. You cannot grow up in a society such as ours—which pretends to believe in a beneficent God and a happy afterlife, yet fears death above all and even considers it the ultimate evil—without having extreme reactions to it.

Some of us went out to his family's place, about an hour's drive away, to say good-bye to him in the last days of his life. On the way back the traffic was horrible, and we'd already talked about having some lunch at Alpine Village, where we'd all met to carpool, before going back to work. I mentioned that—because we were passing Little India on the way back and because the traffic was so bad—we might as well get off the freeway for a while and have some Indian food.

We were tired and emotionally wrung out, so we did just that. We went to an excellent Indian buffet. And we all tucked into that Indian food like a pack of starving wolves. Even the perfect size 6 among us piled her plate high.

When I got home that night I realized what had really been going on.

There was Shiva, god of death, on his altar in my bedroom, which now that I'd gotten rid of all the sexual imagery left him with just his death imagery. We had just eaten the food of his people among his people. Shiva had clearly been trying to get a message to me, and I was so upset about my relationship or lack of same that I hadn't heard or seen it. He was trying to tell me that I was going to need him to deal with the situation, and he was also probably trying to give me a heads-up that there was something more important on tap for me that week than my relationship's break-up. Our group's buffet encounter had been an affirmation of our lives, and a reminder that in the midst of death we needed to keep up our strength for those who would need us. Appreciating that food was an appreciation of life, and the fact that we still could enjoy it.

I had offered to pay for lunch, but the others insisted on chipping in. Most times no one objects when someone else wants to pay the tab, but in this case I think everyone was giving a monetary "offering," whether they were conscious of it or not.

That takes care of Shiva, but what about Venus? Well, the snow globe had a miniature of the Venus de Milo in it. As you know, the unreconstructed statue has its arms missing, of course. Should one go into a relationship un-armed? Wouldn't that give too much power to the other party in the relationship? The symbolism struck me as being overwhelming—how had I not noticed it before? In a relationship the two parties need to be equal, and going into it being "well and whole" is the best situation to be in. I really didn't need that snow globe. I wasn't rejecting Venus; I was rejecting her in a form that was not whole and therefore did not represent the goddess as she should be and did not represent the kind of relationship I'd like to have.

So if you are mad at the gods, feel free to yell, swear, or throw things. Why not get a stick and go beat on the ocean? You can't hurt it by doing that, and you'll eventually tire yourself out so much that you won't be so angry anymore.

Chapter 5
That 4-Letter Word: Work

Affirmations

At work, I am respected and valued.

☙❧

In my career, I am successful and revered.

☙❧

At work, the God/dess works through me.

☙❧

The gods approve of and aid me in my work.

My dad has always maintained that the world's worst four-letter work is work. For many people this would appear to be true! But although we joke about it a lot, it's true that our working lives aren't always as pleasant as we'd want them to be. And that's when we need our spirituality and oftentimes our magick the most.

I happen to believe that it is at our chosen work that we manifest divinity the most. It is there that we have the greatest opportunity to do the deities' work, to represent a positive example of a Wiccan or pagan, and to affect the greatest number of people at one time in a positive way. The only other area in which we affect people so dramatically is what we do while we are amongst our loved ones.

Most pagans and Wiccans I know have some token of their belief at work. Now before we get into the politics of having pentagrams and such at the office, let's remember what our symbols really are: a flower, a leaf, a stone, a shell—these are all manifestations of our beliefs, for ours is a nature-based religion.

Also, I cannot emphasize too strongly the need to stay connected to nature while at work. Although many Wiccans and pagans do work in earth-centered professions such as animal or child care, farming, gardening, and environmental work, for most of the rest of us "work" means pushing paper in a building that has little to do with the natural world and whose windows may not even open.

For example, I am a college instructor. I make it a point to walk outside whenever possible between classes; college campuses are filled with natural wonders. For example, one school where I teach has a whole warren of bunny rabbits on campus, families of ducks, and even the occasional guinea pig. The other school where I work is next to a nature preserve, so our wildlife includes skunks, opossums, squirrels, raccoons, hawks, foxes, and, nowadays, off campus in the nature preserve's lake, an alligator! Could I be more lucky than to have all this wildlife around me, right as I step outside the classroom? We also have autumn leaves, flowering peach trees, ravens, birds of paradise plants, roses, banana trees, wild parrots, and other exotic items that Mother Nature or her minions the landscapers have stirred into the mix of Southern California flora and fauna.

Yet I somehow manage to continue to be a pain and complain to myself and anyone who will listen about my petty grievances with the workplace! For example…

Grading Papers

Well, I was all ticked off about something, who knows what—I can't remember right now and I'm sure it was nothing significant. I was sitting there wondering, *If the Mayan calendar ends in 2012 does that mean I can stop grading papers, like, right now?* I was very unhappy with the state of my career, bitter about my age being a factor in obtaining a tenured position, on and on and on. I promise not to bore you with this. Ah, there goes the landlady, and then I also become angry that my rent is so high and my pay so low.

Suddenly I had a thought: Why was I focused on everything else but what was going on around me at the time? At the time I was sitting outdoors at a picnic table in the apartment complex where I live. It was a lovely spring day, warm with a cool breeze off the ocean. Wind chimes tinkled in the air, and flowers were in bloom. I was not ill; I had food to eat and my rent was paid; nature was all around me, and no one or nothing was bothering me.

So how dare I be so cranky and unhappy! I thought of those who have so much less than I do and figured that many people would love to be sitting at a table beneath a beach umbrella on a beautiful Southern California day with nothing more strenuous to do than grade essays. For once, I really *saw* nature around me, with its beauty and its blessings. For once I was *grateful* for having those papers to grade, and for my work to allow me to do what I need to do in such a pleasant place.

Think about this incident the next time you are angry or unhappy with your work. What could you do to make your day more congenial? Is there anything happening *right this minute* to upset you, or is steam still coming out of your ears over a cross word the boss said last week? If you still have trouble with this concept, go back to Chapter 3. Stay in the moment. It is the only thing we really know for sure is real.

Now, what about those pentagrams in the workplace? I know people who wear them at their jobs. One good friend is a social worker; I have to think her pentagram is a warning to those group homes she visits not to lie to her about the care being given to young people in those places. Others who have government jobs exercise their freedom of religion and wear them.

I generally don't. That doesn't mean I don't wear my Isis pendant or other Egyptian or goddess jewelry—I do. But the pentagram raises fear and ire in people that images of most gods and goddesses do not…with a few exceptions.

Well, there's Cernunnos, for example. Of course I can wear a Shiva pendant, Ganesh, Thoth, Osiris, Horus, Diana, Hathor, and so forth. But not Cernunnos or another horned god. Why? Because to many people he symbolizes the devil. Yes, the Christian devil got his horns from the various horned deities of pre-Christian times, and he got his pitchfork from deities such as Shiva and Poseidon (though most people don't know that about Shiva; representations of Hindu deities and Buddha are usually respected by others in this multicultural age.) The devil also got his forked tail and red coloring from composite deities such as Set.

Of course I feel angry that I don't feel comfortable wearing images of some of the deities of my ancestors. And it makes me angry that I'm uncomfortable wearing my Thor's hammer pendant, either, as some might mistake it for an anti-Semitic symbol, which it certainly is not.

But look at the progress that HAS been made: I have overwhelmingly positive reactions to my Egyptian jewelry; people love Egyptian designs—just look at the popularity of the new King Tut exhibit! Right now in addition to that exhibit another Southern California museum is exhibiting some of the Egyptian mummies from the British Museum.

I started getting a rep as someone who was positive toward Egyptians—students from Egypt started attending my classes! Considering the bad press that people from Arabic countries are getting right now, it meant a lot to them that someone viewed aspects of their culture positively.

I never tell my students or employers that I am an Isian or pagan, but if they ask I won't lie. And I don't often get a negative reply. Most are curious about what our beliefs entail, and it sometimes encourages "broom-closeted" students to open up about their own spirituality.

But back to work. Yes, it's giant pain in the butt, I know, and not because of the work itself most times. Usually it's other people and their reactions that make work a hellish place. So magickally you need more than just a "Get a Job" spell—you need magick for protection above all.

Usually it's not our own behavior that gets us in trouble at work. It's usually the reactions of others. There might be someone who just doesn't like you and rats to the boss about you every time you make a personal call or stay on coffee break for two extra minutes. There might be someone who is jealous of your accomplishments on the job and who sets out to sabotage your career. Indeed, there have been whole books written on the subject of dealing with difficult people at work.

First, I'd like to refer you back to Chapter 2 if you haven't read it yet as well as Chapter 1, both of which offer some tips for magickally dealing with others and the workplace. Then I'd like to refer you to my spellwork in *The Dark Archetype*, which gives quite a few ritual suggestions for a successful career. But here I'll outline the most important everyday things you can do at work to make it all work out.

I hope you'll excuse my humor here; I am using some phrases you might have seen on potions in the botanicas, because I find them highly appropriate and also funny!

The Boss Fix

No, this doesn't mean getting him neutered. (Although that might help!) It means "fixing" him so that he isn't "fixated" on whatever mistakes you make or those he imagines you make. This can encompass many, many issues regarding the workplace, but I'll take one a couple of the most common ones here.

Credit Where Credit Is Due

How many times has your boss taken credit for your ideas? What solutions have you come up with that suddenly sound as though your boss figured them out all by himself? Well, if this is happening to you, it can not only impact your self-esteem and morale on the job, but it can also cost you in terms of cold, hard cash when it comes to listing your accomplishments when you go for a promotion or a job at another company. So you want to nip that in the bud right now.

Get a bottle of *Boss fix* oil. Dress a white tea or votive candle with it. Now repeat the following affirmation before, during, and after you light the candle:

My name shall be known
My ideas shall be acknowledged
My contributions shall be recognized.

Repeat at least nine times. If you have read *The Dark Archetype* you might want to follow some of the directions for invoking Oya. If you haven't, then simply get a picture of Oya from a botanica or off the web. Place it next to the candle. Then write the boss's name on a piece of paper and place it under the candle.

Now appeal to Oya:

Hekua, Oya of the winds,
I appeal to you to give me
Credit where credit is due.
That is all I am asking,
Great goddess Oya,
Thank you.

If you want to, take the paper out from under the candle. Write your name over it three times, until the boss's name is unreadable. Then say the following:

The universe gives me credit
For my accomplishments.
I am rewarded in many ways
For all that I do.

That's it. Let the candle burn, or, if you have to leave, burn it a little each time you're home until it's done.

What if the boss lies about you or your accomplishments? It's been known to happen, for a variety of reasons. Perhaps the boss doesn't want to give you credit for what you've done because then he'd have to give you a raise. Maybe he has, in fact, lied about you to his superiors, for whatever reason; who knows why bosses do what they do? Anyway, start with the candle and *Boss fix* oil. If you have a statue or a picture of Sekhmet, place it on the altar with the candle, then say this:

I shine with the light
Of Sekhmet,
Righteous warrior,
Avenging lioness.
May I shine with your light
In the eyes of my employers.

If you have worked with Oya or Sehkmet in this way, it would be nice to offer her a glass of good red wine as thanks.

If the boss just needs "fixing" in general rather than for a specific reason—let's say she's done so much to tick you and the other workers off that it'd take you all day to list her bad deeds, then try the following.

Anoint a black candle with the *Boss fix* oil. Now we're going to invoke Ma'at, the Egyptian goddess whose very name means "truth." And if you think she's not as scary as Oya or Sekhmet, then watch out! The truth will out, as they say.

Once you have anointed the candle, get a feather to place next to it as a symbol of Ma'at. Then say the following:

Oh Ma'at,
Let the truth
Be known
And all falsehoods
Blow away
Like shifting desert sands
Covering all untruths.

Tell Ma'at what the problem is. She's a good listener; it's her job. And while I can't promise that you'll go to work the next day and find your boss sitting up to his neck in a sand dune in his office, you can expect that his lies will decrease and if they don't, those who are his bosses will soon learn of his untruths and take appropriate action.

Now for another situation that may come up at work, whether boss-related or not:

That Hoodoo That They Do

Suspect you've got a hoodoo man or woman at work? Well, if he or she's good at it, you probably *won't* suspect them at all! There are things you can do to protect yourself by using a little hoodoo of your own. First of all, let's take another trip to the botanica, and get the following oils:

- Run, devil, run
- Has no *hanna*

That 4-Letter Word: Work

- Jinx breaker or Hex breaker
- Just judge

Here's how we'll use them. If you think someone at work is after your job, spreading gossip about you, or trying to sabotage your work in any way, then you need the *Run, devil, run* oil. We're going to do an old-fashioned warding, a type of spell you might not have seen except maybe on *Buffy the Vampire Slayer!* Think of a "ward" as an invisible guard dog: It's stronger than just protection; it keeps someone out of your business. Now, ordinarily in hoodoo, we could place some ground brick dust across the entrance to your office or cubicle to keep them out. But that's a little obtrusive, so let's try this instead.

Take a tissue and dampen it with a bit of the oil. Make a circuit of your workspace and place a dab of it in each corner; rub it in well (it won't hurt anything). Now also put a dab on your own belongings—you car, your purse, even your coat if you hang it up and leave it in your personal space. As you do so, visualize your office and your things as being warded by whatever symbol works for you—perhaps a big black dog, such as Anubis, say, or an invisible security guard with an itchy trigger finger! Do this on a monthly basis.

At the same time, take stock of your possessions and who has access to them. The hoodoo practitioner can make mischief with little things—a few hairs from your brush or the back of your coat; any nail parings or even the fingernail dust from a nail file; a pen or pencil you may have chewed on; a few drops of saliva from a toothbrush if you keep one at work. The idea is to keep people from having access to anything that comes directly from your body.

Sound superstitious? Well, only until someone's worked a hoodoo on you; then you'll be surprised and a little bit scared. Best be safe rather than sorry.

What if you do really believe someone has worked a spell on you? Then you need the *Jinx breaker* oil or *Hex breaker* oil. You'll need to wash or clean any clothing or other items you have at work that might have been vulnerable. Put a couple of drops of the oil in the wash water. Then take a spray bottle of whatever you clean your desk or other equipment with, place a few drops in that, and clean up! Look for anything suspicious; pull out the drawers in the desk and look underneath. Find anything there? Maybe a feather or coin or some other object either taped below the drawer or stuck in the back of it. Then again, maybe you have seen some dusty material at the entrance to your workspace. Hmmm. Could be a hex.

Now don't get too worried. We're not talking heavy-duty black magick that someone's done to you; just clean your space and think positive thoughts. If you suddenly find someone coming around to your office more often than usual when this is happening, you can probably suspect that person. Just smile and keep cleaning.

Sometimes the boss plays favorites. He or she may be, in fact, playing around a little too much with a subordinate and letting that person have all the perqs. Now you need the *Has no hanna* oil, or, as they say in the LBC, "has no Heina." Well, usually everyone knows when the boss is sleeping with his secretary, and it's never good for business and can interfere with your own progress at work. This one's a little tricky to do because you have to get into the boss's space to do it. If you can't do so, well, there's always his car out in the parking lot....

Anyway, if you can, place some of the oil in a place where he'll put his hands, such as the arms of his chair or the handle of the door. You can do this to his car, too. Now, if you know who the other party is (as I said, it's probably obvious), do the same thing there. Both of them should become a bit reticent about touching each other and perhaps the whole affair will begin to cool off and things will get back to normal.

When you come up for a performance evaluation it doesn't hurt to use some *Just judge* oil to see that you are evaluated fairly. Use it liberally; if you have to fill out any forms, make sure just a bit is on them. If you shake hands with the evaluator, you'd better have some on your hands. Keep your mind open and a positive thought.

Recipes for Success

Now here are a few recipes for success.

Mix the following ingredients:

Equal parts *Success* oil, *Get a job* oil, *Fast luck* oil, *Steady work* oil, and so on. Rub this on the palm of your hands when you go for a job interview or a performance evaluation, or when you are up for a promotion.

Alternately, in a bit of carrier oil such as jojoba or even baby oil, mix a few drops of essential oils of cinnamon, cedar, and ginger OR basil, oregano, and rosemary. Test a drop on your skin first to make sure you're not allergic. Dilute them really well or they will smell too strongly. Use as directed previously.

There are many ways to use magick to make the workplace a better place. Get inspired to start your own business, do a creative project, or find a new career by mixing in a diffuser an equal amount of essential oils of lemon, orange, mandarin, lime, ginger, and vetiver. Inhale the wonderful scent and let the creativity flow!

Another fun way to suss out what's going on at work is to train yourself to see and interpret people's auras. See Chapter 7 for ways to begin.

Take heart: No matter how bad a job situation is, there IS always another job out there somewhere for you. Think in a limited fashion and you will find your life limited in many ways. Think expansively and eventually your happiness at work as well as your bank account will expand accordingly!

Chapter 6
In Sickness and in Health: Yours and Others

Affirmations

I am well and whole.
I am well and strong.
I am healthy and able.
I am a successful organism.

"I am a successful WHAT?" you may say. Well, here's my story.

The Homeopath

On a visit to the gynecologist I was diagnosed with a benign ovarian cyst. The doctor wanted to operate, but I of course save my episodes of slice-and-dice for life-threatening events, not benign physical SNAFUs. I told her I wanted to go to an alternative practitioner instead, and she said, "Okay, but if the cyst isn't gone in a couple of months I'm going to take it out."

I went to a homeopathic doctor. These doctors treat the patient holistically, so he asked me about my medical history in addition to my current complaint. After I rattled off a litany of aches, pains, and minor traumas, he wrote it all down, then stopped.

"You're a successful organism," he said.

"Say what?" I asked.

He looked at my chart again. "You're a successful organism. By that I mean that since you have reached the age of 40 without any major health problems such as cancer, heart disease, or diabetes, you are fundamentally a successful organism. If you weren't, you wouldn't have attained your current age to begin with. Now take these pills and see if the cyst goes away, and stop worrying."

It felt good to know that I was fundamentally strong and sound, despite whatever health "issues" I felt like complaining about. I decided that I liked the "successful organism" idea, and included it in my affirmations. I hope you will, too.

Oh, yeah, and the next time I saw the gynecologist, I didn't need the operation, because the cyst was gone.

Now let's say them again:

I am well and whole.
I am well and strong.
I am healthy and able.
I am a successful organism.

But what if you're not "well" and "whole"? We'll get to that. First read this story, a sort of cautionary tale.

A Misogynist by Any Other Name

Some famous female doctor who shall remain nameless had the incredibly idiotic idea that creativity is linked to the uterus! (So, uh, I guess that means men can't be creative?) Well, one of my closest friends had a hysterectomy and, unfortunately, she had read this woman's book. Afterwards, she not only no longer felt "well and whole," even though the operation improved her physical health tremendously, but she also bought into this doctor's idea and therefore felt that her creativity was gone because her uterus was gone!

She also cried at any ritual when a woman was spoken of as a "womb-man" or other supposedly pro-female idea, or when she was supposed to "see the color orange in the area of your womb" during a chakra meditation.

It is totally antithetical to the women's movement to define a woman by her womb, and the fact that so-called pro-women doctors and supposedly spiritual people would do so is very hurtful. My friend has every right to feel "well and whole" without her womb.

Do I feel somehow lacking because I no longer have an appendix or a gall bladder? Am I less of a woman or less than creative because of this? Hell no! What a ludicrous idea. My point is not to buy into antiquated ideas. They may be coming from the mouth of some New Ager, but if so then the New Ager is obviously channeling some old misogynist.

So repeat the affirmations as often as you like, even if you don't feel whole, strong, or particularly "successful" as an organism or anything else. See if they make a change in your outlook. I'm betting they will and, as anyone who knows me will tell you, I'm a pretty shrewd gambler.

Now let's do some heavy lifting on a weighty issue.

The Diagnosis

When someone very dear to me was diagnosed with a terminal disease, I did what everyone would expect from a priestess, professor, and practitioner of good critical thinking: I completely fell apart. I dissolved into a little puddle of tiger butter. I hit the wall the way a soap opera diva turning 40 would. I crumbled as if an L.A. freeway in an earthquake. You get the idea—I think I was even more upset than the person with the illness!

For a time I completely forgot about Isis, Hygeia, Thoth, Obatala, Kwan Yin, the Medicine Buddha, and all the other gods and goddesses of medicine, healing, and compassion to whom I should have turned. I was so out of it that I think at one point Loki put on his Doc Martens and kicked my ass in order to get me to WAKE UP and do what I was supposed to be doing.

I should have remembered the best advice from the late, great Douglas Adams:

DON'T PANIC.

(Come to think of it, maybe it was Pan who left those bruises on my derriere.)

"First, you cry," is the appropriate way to begin, as is simply but elegantly stated by award-winning journalist Betty Rollin in her book when she was diagnosed with breast cancer. First, you cry; then, you talk to Deity.

In this chapter you will find simple prayers, affirmations, actions to take, and hopefully some support in this time of troubles. Take heart. We are all living in it, this Time of Troubles, which the Hindus call the Kali Yuga. So in the spirit of the times let's start with Kali's hottie, Shiva, shall we? This is a procedure that is heavy-duty and that may be performed in times of life-and-death situations; if you don't need it right now, skip it and go on to The Isis Prayer.

Shiva, Baby

As I've stated before, I keep a Shiva altar in my bedroom. Shiva is a god of BIG THINGS, and I'm not just talking about his, er, lingam. He is a dealer in big endings and big beginnings, and so it's no wonder he's thought of as a god of both sex and death.

If the situation is life-threatening, or may become so, appeal to Shiva. I suggest buying an inexpensive picture of him, which can be found in virtually any New Age store, head shop, or Hindu-owned shop. Shiva has dreadlocks and grayish or bluish skin. Pictured with him will most likely be a lingam, which is supposed to represent a stylized penis but which actually resembles one of those 3-foot-high barriers that are erected (ahem) to keep burglars and terrorists from running their pick-up trucks into buildings. Get a good look at one of those and keep its image in your head.

At home or in another safe space bow to Shiva and say his prayer at least three times:

Ohm Namah Shivaya.

Prostrate yourself and place your forehead on the floor if you are physically able to do so, and say his prayer three times. Ask Shiva to have mercy on the unwell individual, and ask that if the illness is incurable ask Shiva to help make the person's transition to the other side an easy one. Also ask him to help you cope. Write it down as a petition if you wish and offer it to him with a bowl of milk and some mixed nuts.

During this difficult time, look for lingam-shaped objects in your daily life. Whenever you see one, say:

Ohm Namah Shivaya.

When you see a bright red hibiscus, whether real or on a Hawaiian-print shirt, say it. When you pass a shop that sells lingerie or "adult toys," say it. When you see a display of bananas and mangoes in the supermarket, say it. When you pass a cemetery or funeral home, say it.

Laugh when you see a symbol of Shiva! Someone will wonder why you're giggling over a package of pistachio nuts at Trader Joe's, or smiling at the hibiscus-print shirt of one of its employees. Smile when you see a fire hydrant, especially a red one! If you can find time, read Norman Cousins's book, *Anatomy of an Illness*, in which he describes how he cured himself of a serious illness with virtually nothing but Vitamin C and some Marx Brothers comedies. Laughter, if has been said, can be thought of as "internal jogging." It literally gives your insides a workout. More fun and easier on the joints that real jogging, I say.

Continue the practice while the illness continues. Thank Shiva with a mango-scented candle and sandalwood incense when the crisis passes. Remember that Shiva is always with you if you need him. That's why his altar is in my bedroom.

I've needed him a lot lately.

If you'll oblige me, I'll tell you one more tale.

Dying With Dignity, Albeit Unlawfully

He was in great need of medical marijuana. It was the only thing that helped ease the pain and nausea of his terminal illness. I was a friend of his niece, a nice middle-aged librarian who had never "done drugs" in her life. He was a retired Catholic priest, her uncle, and he was dying of cancer. It was against his beliefs to break the law, but it was also against his beliefs to end his pain by ending his own life, and so he was faced with a terrible choice: offend his country by obtaining marijuana illegally or offend his God by taking his own life in order to end his pain.

Needless to say, he chose the former, though he felt very guilty about both breaking the law and the necessity his niece was now faced with: purchasing the forbidden substance from sleazy drug dealers.

Thankfully, this would probably not happen now, for, although the wheels of justice move exceedingly slowly, marijuana has now been approved for certain medical uses in several states, including California. I will pray to Shiva—for whom marijuana is a sacred herb—in memory of my friend's uncle and fellow sufferers who deserve to die with dignity and without suffering.

Let's face it: Many of us do not feel "well and whole" a lot of the time. For some, pain is a constant companion. For others, various disabilities make everyday chores difficult. Still others of us may live in the shadow of the Reaper, with only our new god—Modern Medicine—keeping us alive. So how do we endure?

Keep up your affirmations, first of all. Define "well and whole" any way you see fit. It is not for others to judge or to define you or your situation. Resist our society's habit of labeling anything; create your own labels, if you wish. If you want to call yourself "differently abled," that's fine. I just call myself a cripple and let it go at that, but then I have a sick sense of humor.

Maybe we should heed the wisdom of the Dalai Lama and get over the idea that our lives need to be perfect all the time. If we go with his hypothesis, then we accept that there is suffering in life and can then get on with our happy hour. Is it five o'clock yet?

Here's a special prayer for times of illness, pain, or discomfort, or when you do the brilliant things I do, such as falling down flights of stairs.

The Isis Prayer

This is an extremely simple prayer that you can use any time you are ill, whether it be a minor tension headache from sitting in meetings all day or a major illness that has you sidelined. You don't even have to speak it aloud. I use it every time I am ill or in pain, whether major or minor. Here it is:

Isis Attend Me
Isis Mend Me

Say it at least three times, or repeat it over and over to yourself, or aloud. When I wake up achy in the morning I say it in the shower; when I am lying down with a bad headache I say it as I'm going to sleep. It's the easiest prayer to remember, and it states its point simply and easily, using the active voice. Let's say it again:

Isis Attend Me
Isis Mend Me

That's all there is to it. If I say it while lying down, I imagine Isis standing by my bedside, hands in the familiar position of blessing with palms up and toward me, almost as though she were giving me a Reiki treatment. If you are standing or sitting, imagine Isis behind you, wrapping her wings around you as though a warm shawl. Feel the healing power of her hands and wings. Continue to visualize if you can and breathe deeply, saying or thinking the Isis Prayer as often as you like.

Some may object to this prayer being written in the imperative, which is the type of sentence indicating a command or request. I say, get to the heart of the matter. When you need help, you need it *now*. Remember that trust goes both ways with deities: You must trust the deities to understand what you need and to not be offended because you did not couch your request in an overly formal or obsequious manner.

And remember on your good days to thank the deities. The Iseum of Isis Paedusis recently celebrated Mabon, the witches' Thanksgiving. This year we gave thanks not only for the plenty in our lives—but we also gave thanks for a dear friend who had just passed over. We remembered her with great joy and expressed our appreciation of her and the privilege it was having her in our lives. It made a difference. Of course there is time for rending of garments and wringing of hands after a loved one passes, but there is also the thought of thanksgiving for knowing that person in the first place. Give thanks to the gods for what you have, and what you have had in the past if you have it no more.

So let's say some more affirmations:

I thank the goddess for this day.

༄

I thank the gods for my memories.

༄

I thank the deities for all that I have been given in life, whether I still have it or not.

༄

I am truly blessed by the gods.

You can then thank the gods for anything specific you care to mention.

Healing is one of the main reasons we look to our deities. We pray for a specific outcome to an operation or to a medical test; we pray that once we hear the outcome we will be able to cope with it and do whatever needs to be done if it is not the outcome we had hoped for. Most of all, we realize that the deities are indeed there for us, and therefore we are never truly alone.

That is a great comfort for most people and I hope it will be for you, too. Sometimes, however, people abandon their gods during the bad times. They feel the gods have let them down. Go back to the Kwan Yin working if you feel this way. Kwan Yin weeps for all her children who suffer. She has never deserted them, and we have no indication that she ever will. As long as there is suffering, she will be with us.

Take comfort by using the methods our people have always used—although we might have called them by other names from time to time throughout the centuries! Aromatherapy, massage, laying on of hands, Reiki, meditation, guided visualization, therapeutic baths—the list is endless. Sometimes all you need are some Epsom salts, a drop or two of lavender oil, and some hot water, and you have yourself a healing bath. Just think: Nowadays our health insurance covers such treatments as chiropractic, acupuncture, and other physical therapy modalities, naturopathy, even biofeedback! Earlier generations might have called these practitioners "witch doctors," but their methods are now recognized by science as being effective for a lot of conditions. Witch doctors—if they only knew….

Not everyone has health insurance—something our country should be really ashamed of. So there are other ways to cover the costs of alternative treatments. Barter is one way; what service or product could you offer in return for treatments? I am a big proponent of using barter in the Wiccan/pagan community as a way to serve our community better and make life easier for us all. Sometimes you have to get creative to get the treatment you need. Networking with other groups and persons of our belief systems can only strengthen our community and serve to help each other in it.

Probably the best way to deal with health problems is to prevent them in the first place. I've already spoken earlier in the book about eating right and exercising. Well, you don't have to join an expensive gym; go for a walk. You don't have to buy designer food; go to a local farmer's market for fresher and cheaper organic produce.

And learn to keep stress from killing you! Meditate for a few minutes every day; do the recommended exercises in Chapter 7. Enlist support from friends and family. Walk with a neighbor. Ask friends to come over once a week on a weeknight to meditate. Go grocery shopping with your significant other. Play with a pet or the kids. These are all simple healing modalities and we, sadly, don't usually recognize them as such.

I see whole groups of senior citizens walking in the mall in the mornings—they're power-walking, but not outdoors when it's too hot or too rainy. Sounds great to me! It's also common to see people exercising in the park or at the beach. Why not? If you do so you're adding the benefits of nature to your workout, even if it's just a few chi gong stretches!

Here's a healing technique I learned from W. E. Butler in his book, *How to Read the Aura*: Recharge your batteries by leaning on a tree! Yes, that idea I've been promoting can even help you gain energy when you're tired and it feels that the world has sucked all the life out of you. Just find a nice tree and sit with your back against it. Butler prefers pine trees, and warns against elm trees, but I'm not sure what he has against elms!

You may have read that Benjamin Franklin used to take "air baths." Well, this story varies a bit depending on where you heard it or read it, but the idea is to air out your skin and let the pores of you body breathe, for heaven's sake! That means you have to get naked, something we do very infrequently. Even now, late at night at home alone, I'm sitting here shackled in my underwire bra, pullover sweater, pants, socks, and undies. Why, exactly? So that if there's a major earthquake I won't be caught without my Maidenform bra? Most of you are probably too young to remember those wonderfully suggestive Maidenform ads. My favorite: "I dreamed I took the bull by the horns in my Maidenform bra." Get those clothes off and let your skin breathe!

There. I took most of those things off and put on my fuzzy pink robe. Is that too much information?

Anyway, back to the air baths. It's a good idea to brush your aura or have a close (very close) friend do so. Our aura extends a few inches out from our bodies; some say much farther. Aura-brushing is similar to smudging in its intent. Why not alternate doing both?

Now it may not seem too healthy to you folks in northern climes to be running around in the house nude, let alone asking your significant other to "come in here and brush my aura."

In any case, why not steam up the bathroom real well and have a hot shower, dry off, and then sit in this "steam room," with a couple of drops of eucalyptus, lavender, rosemary, fir, or birch oil in the diffuser? Then take your "air bath" and have someone brush your aura, or do it yourself with a bath brush. Needless to say, if you have access to a sauna or steam room, make good use of it. Most world cultures have seen sauna and its relatives as sacred, healing spaces. Remember when President Clinton went to Russia? He was asked to join Russian President Yeltsin in the sauna. There Yeltsin pelted him with birch branches—an ancient form of initiation. It's nice to know some pagan practices have made it into modern times!

Whenever I am in a sauna I always say a prayer to the Finnish deities, Tapio and Meilikki, the god and goddess of the sauna. The sauna as we know it is the product of indigenous Finnish culture, where it came from the people we call the Laplanders, but who call themselves Saami. Whenever I am at a health club and use the sauna I say a silent prayer of thanks to Tapio and Meilikki for the healing properties of the sauna, and I also pray for the good health of all the other people in the club. I will speak the prayers aloud if I'm alone.

I also feel that one of the best things you can do for your health is to help others. Take some of the previous suggestions: Ask a neighbor to join you for a walk; take a friend to the health club with you; join a friend at the beach or park; or have a "do-it-yourself sauna night" with the girls and turn your bathroom into a makeshift sauna and brush each other's auras, if only because you know it would piss off the religious right!

But hey, I'm getting political. Well, the personal IS political, isn't it? And what should we do about our health and politics? Well, Dr. Andrew Weil and others suggest we take a "news fast" every now and then to help with stress. What, did you think you would hear GOOD news on CNN? Or on any other channel? A news fast is a good idea if you are under terrible stress. However, being politically active does mean keeping up with the news and being active in that way may actually help your health if it makes you feel good to participate. What's good for the soul is good for the body, after all.

While the girls are over, why not have a health evening and treat each other to avocado facials, health drinks, and the like? Yeah, I'll give up happy hour and give myself a facial and make a health drink, and when I finish this book I'm never going to eat fast food again because I don't have time to prepare myself a decent meal!

See what we writers sacrifice for the greater good? Hey, put down that hamburger and make yourself a pomegranate smoothie!

But seriously, let's go back to the idea of prayer as a means of keeping healthy. It's a long tradition, and we can think of prayer as a mantrum (yes, that's the singular of *mantra*. The most famous of course is simply *ohm mani padme hum*. Many feminists chant *Om Ma*, as those two syllables take the voice all the way from the back of the throat out onto the lips and glorify the goddess. Whatever you choose to chant or prayer you choose to say, say it with love and jubilation, and say it for your health.

The best thing you can do is keep up with the latest health news, and read books by positive practitioners who have a healthy respect for both traditional and alternative medicine. Your local library can help you find the books you're interested in and will most likely have the newest, most popular and well-reviewed books. Be careful with Internet sources; you never know what information is correct.

Remember that we are not just rainbow bodies and spirits yearning to breathe free—we also have these meat constructs we call "bodies" to take care of, and if we don't, nobody else will.

Now go read the award-winning story "They're Made Out of Meat" by Terry Bisson. You need a good laugh; I can tell.

Chapter 7

Everyday Magick

Dianne Sylvan, in her book *The Circle Within*, states that "…making magick is a religious act that must be considered in the context of our relationship with Deity…."

I am always surprised to meet people who practice magick yet have no relationship with the gods or profess atheism. To me, we are part and parcel of the gods and no magick really takes place without them. So, although this is a separate chapter from those concerned with our spiritual focus, it is not without the presence of Deity. After all, remember the saying: "Thou art god/dess."

At the beginning of this book I said that you didn't have to go out and buy a lot of stuff in order to do the work herein. I meant that. So, as a Priestess of Thoth and therefore a gambler, I'll bet you that you have at least 75 percent of the items that follow in your home already. So grab this list and check the kitchen and bathrooms for the following:

- White candles—tapers, votives, or tea candles
- Sea salt or kosher salt
- Rubbing alcohol
- Witch hazel
- Epsom salts
- Castor oil
- Matches or a cigarette lighter
- Basil, mint, parsley, sage, rosemary, thyme, or other green herbs
- Cinnamon, ginger, nutmeg, cloves, allspice, or pumpkin pie spice
- Black pepper, red pepper, chili peppers
- Coffee, tea
- Cow's milk or goat's milk
- Beer or wine
- Oranges, apples, bananas
- Roses or rose water, cologne, essential oil, or lotion
- Sugar or honey
- Spring water or distilled water

So, okay, how'd you do? Did I win the bet? Well, if I did then you have to buy the book!

But anyway, this is a fairly standard list of magickal ingredients that sounds very similar to a traditional shopping list. Remember that our foremothers (and fathers) made magick with what they had; few if any could run off to Tibet to get yak butter or some other exotic ingredient for their spells. (Does anyone use yak butter in spells or did I just make that up?) And it's rare that they had any special ritual tools except what they used for cooking. That's where the often-pejorative term *kitchen witch* comes from, and we need to take back that term as a badge of honor. All that are really needed for magick are intent and will, really; everything else is a prop to amplify the intent.

Now before I start sounding a bit too similar to G. Gordon Liddy let me say that though, yes, magick is effected through concentrating and amplifying one's will until the thought becomes the thing, I will admit that you need more than that to bake a cake and most of us need more than that to make a spell. Basic ingredients, then, are required, but highly specific ingredients are not. Yes, I like black, patchouli-scented candles at Samhain, but I don't believe that my dearly departed really give a flying fig what color candles I use when the veil between the worlds is thin.

So. For the basic Wiccan-style altar you need to represent the elements, so there's your water, salt, herbs to burn as incense or a spritz of rosewater if you prefer, and candles to light. There you go.

Here's a simple house blessing incense recipe I got back in the 1980s from the proprietors of Botanica Ogun in Lennox, California:

2 Tbsp. sugar

Zest of an orange (or some dried orange peel)

A cinnamon stick (ground cinnamon can substitute)

Some rose petals or rose incense

Mix and then place about a teaspoon of the mixture on some lit charcoal to "sweeten" up the dispositions of those in the household. If you've got commercial House Blessing or a similar incense around you can add it to the mix as well, but it's not necessary.

See how easy that was?

Most of us also make offerings to deities when we work with them in our magick, and these can be simple, too. Apples can be offered to most European deities; oranges to Asian and Middle Eastern ones; bananas for New World deities, Shiva, or any other "horny" god. Milk is a fine offering to Egyptian, Norse, Hindu, and Celtic gods. Beer is good for Norse, Slavic, Egyptian, and Celtic deities. Wine is for Greeks, Romans, and general use. Spring or purified water is preferred by Afro-Latin deities and can substitute for any other liquid offering—with one exception. During the time that I was writing this passage I went to a lecture and meditation given by Dr. David Williams, a British pathologist and Egyptologist. He stated that Anubis, for one, does not appreciate the "pure spring water" that so many folks seem to want to offer the deities. It appears that Anubis wants his beer or wine, so obviously I was meant to heed this advice and pass it along! For a listing of more extensive offerings, see Chapter 4.

Now look at that list again. Here are some more examples of ways to use the items on the list in your everyday magick:

- Stir hot, sweet spices into your coffee or tea and you're adding prosperity, fame, and sex appeal. Stir green herbs into your sauces and you're adding abundance, fertility, healing, and—here in America—money.

- Make "witch fire" by pouring a little rubbing alcohol over a handful of Epsom salts in a cauldron or other fireproof container, light it, and poof! Groovy blue flames. Fun at Samhain and any dark moon ritual. The kids will love it.

- Bathe in Epsom salts, sea salt, or kosher salt to draw negativity out of your system (and aches and pains, too). Light a white candle while you're bathing to further purify yourself and the room. Clean your ritual tools, statues, and altar with witch hazel. Use castor oil compresses for various health problems; consult the Edgar Cayce remedy book in Appendix III for ideas.

- Wake yourself up in the morning by smelling black pepper or crushed rosemary leaves. Add red pepper or crushed chilies to your cooking sauces to heat up a relationship. Sprinkle black or red pepper across the neighbors' doorstep if you'd prefer that they and their smelly hounds and their garage band (you get the idea) move on to a more suitable location. Spray rosewater around the bedroom to make it more lovey-dovey. Spray it in the kids' room so they won't fight.

- Keep a permanent altar if you wish; all you need are a rose, a glass of water or milk, and a piece of fruit kept on it at all times. Use honey or sugar to "sweeten" any spell. Sprinkle salt water in all the corners of the house to protect it. Sprinkle green herbs in front of your business to bring in more money. Cut an apple in half and admire the pentagram in its center; slice a starfruit for instant, edible pentagrams. Eat an orange and visualize gold and long life.

The uses of such common ingredients become obvious after you have practiced magick for a while and recognize their individual properties. Although some say that all petitions have to be written on parchment with a quill pen and dragon's blood ink, I say a piece of scratch paper and a ballpoint will work just fine if your intent is clear and your will strong. Some will say it's unlucky to light candles or incense with matches, and I say that's a superstition left over from the days when matches were called Lucifers.

Be like our ancestors and make do. The world is full of easily accessible resources, and our deities expect us to use them wisely. In fact, they'd much prefer we use renewable resources than, say, continue to strip mine the rainforest for quartz crystals.

Back to Basics

Here are some suggestions for magickal tasks that should be completed on a regular basis. I'll leave room for you to add your own; think of it as a magickal "to do" list.

To Do Daily

1. Shield (see "Magick: Fun for the Whole Family," later in this chapter).
2. Connect with the universe and grounding. This is a simple technique that you've not doubt read in numerous books already. Yet it's amazing to me how many of us forget to do it before we attempt any other type of magick. So here it is: Sit in a chair with you feet on the floor, barefoot, if possible. Sit straight but comfortably. Close your eyes and take three deep pranic breaths. Now breathe normally, but imagine the following: As you breathe in, imagine your feet are connected to the earth as though they're the roots of a tree. Breathing in will pull energy up through your legs from the earth. Then when you breathe out, imagine that the top of your head it open to the cosmos. When you exhale, you draw the energy of the stars into your head. When you feel connected to both earth and sky in this way, you are ready to do magick.
3. Meditate or visualize. Get a good meditation tape if you haven't done this before. Practice before doing any of the more complex visualizations in Chapter 4. First, learn "pure" meditation—any tape by the late, great Alan Watts is the purest form, I feel. Then try one of the visualizations in a book—say, Nicki Scully's *The Golden Cauldron*. These visualizations are very

safe and not too difficult. Once you have more experience, go on to lengthier tapes and to the guided visualizations in Chapter 4. Visualization can be used in many ways; many folks visualize themselves as thinner while dieting or visualize themselves in the kind of job they would like to have. See Shakti Gawain's *Creative Visualization*, a primer on this technique, for lots of great suggestions.

4. Generate and utilize energy. See "The Energy Beach Ball" exercise that follows for a fun way to do this.

5. Commune with nature. That's right: Hug a tree. Literally. If you're on you're lunch hour and think your colleagues would look at you oddly (as if they don't already) then no one will think it weird if you sit down on a blanket with your back against a tree and read a book or eat your lunch. And though some of us (well, maybe just Barbara Ardinger and me) feel that our natural habitat is the luxury hotel, the truth of the matter is that we all need to get more familiar with nature and learn Her ways.

Even the grimiest city has greenery somewhere, even if the only flowers to be had must be purchased at a florist's or plucked out of cracks in the concrete. Dr. Andrew Weil states that one way to improve your health is to always have flowers in the house—and hey, he's not even one of us! (Well, maybe he is and doesn't know it, as is the case with many natural-born magicians.) The purpose of interacting with nature is to keep that connection with Gaia and thus with our own true natures. Even if all your magickal supplies come from Indio Products, you need to add an element of real, natural ingredients somewhere along the way.

One of the best ways is to grow some flowers and herbs of your own. Now, I happen to have a notorious "black thumb," so if I grow anything at all I do so outdoors; other apartment dwellers seem to have the magick touch and can grow a few herbs or other indoor plants. (I have found, however, that African violets are indestructible—or maybe it's my harmony with the African deities that keeps them alive; I'm sure they pity me). Plants grown indoors help freshen the air—keep one in your bedroom—and represent another living being, one more naturally attuned to the cosmos than us city folk. Some like to talk to or play classical music around their potted friends in order for them to feel more at home and grow harmoniously.

But what if just a greeting card with a picture of a rose on it makes you break out in hives? One theory of the disorder fibromyalgia (FMS), for example, holds that the salicylates in plants can counteract the main treatment for FMS (namely, guiafenisin). And some people really do have terrible allergies that don't allow them a pleasant time in the wild or even around a bouquet of flowers.

Well, there are other ways to commune with Gaia: stones and shells, for example. I prefer to pick my own that I find in nature even though certainly beautiful crystals are found in most New Age stores, not that these are gathered in the most earth-friendly way, and so I prefer to purchase such stones from "rockhounds" who generally find and polish their own gemstones. Shells can be found in most souvenir shops if you don't have a beach handy, or even just keep those clam, oyster, or mussel shells you get from the fishmonger.

Even wearing certain types of jewelry can keep one in touch with the living Earth. Pearls, of course, are created by the secretions of oysters. Amber is the fossilized remains of tree sap. Coral, also, is a living thing, which is used in jewelry especially by Native Americans. You can also find ammonites and other shells fashioned into jewelry.

Keep that connection with nature consciously in some small way every day. You'll be amazed at the energy that is available just from interacting with it.

6. _____
7. _____
8. _____

To Do Weekly

1. Clear and balance chakras (see instructions following).
2. Clean/rearrange/refresh the altar.

3. Charge charms, amulets, and talismans.
4. _____
5. _____
6. _____
7. _____
8. _____

To Do Monthly

1. Cleanse and purify the home/house blessing.

    One of our seemingly easy magickal tasks is to cleanse our homes of negativity and unwanted visitors—both physical and non-corporeal! Most of us are used to smudging the house, but I'll include a simple method here. Using a sweetgrass or sage bundle or cedar, copal, or dragon's blood incense, first do a banishing. If there has been strife or negativity or you feel a disturbance in the force, so to speak, or the neighbors with the keg parties and the illegal daycare full of shrieking kindergarteners haven't moved, yet you should start this way. Move in a widdershins (counter-clockwise) fashion around the home, smudging the smoke into each part of each room. Repeat the phrase of your choice; for this aspect, you can say, for instance,

    "I banish all negativity from this home. Negativity is not welcome here."

It's best, of course, to write your own specific phrase. Now bless the house by smudging it deosil (clockwise). Say something such as,

"This home is now cleansed of all negativity. I welcome light and love into this home."

Some folks also sprinkle salt water in the corners of the home, and some like to use one of those magickal floor washes that are favored by Latin American *esotericos* and Voudounists and Santeros/Santeras. (See Indio Products for more ideas.)

A hoodoo practitioner I know told me that if you throw a handful of salt into some PineSol and scrub the house with it, that it acts as a banishing/house blessing wash. Now I know why this cleaning product is so popular! I had no idea it had magickal properties.

2. Full moon, new moon, and/or dark moon esbat. An "esbat" is basically any ritual not done on a major sabbat.
3. Prepare for upcoming sabbat.
4. Check and replenish magickal/spiritual supplies.
5. _____
6. _____
7. _____
8. _____

Of course, who am I to say which magickal tasks, studies, or activities you need to do on an ongoing basis? This is just a list of suggestions. The important thing is to have a list of "things to do" or "goals." It needn't be long or complex. Practicing magick is a cumulative endeavor: Any bit that you do builds on another, and so forth. Even if you only fit in one task a day, but actually do that task every day, consider yourself a paragon of magickal virtue!

Magick: Fun for the Whole Family

No doubt you've heard the saying "the family that prays together, stays together." And although that's as true for pagan families as for others, our beliefs have an extra added attraction that can help promote family togetherness: the practice of magick. Now that more and more families are raising their children with pagan or Wiccan beliefs, ways to add elements of those traditions to everyday life can only affect the family positively.

Now, for many, magick is a solitary act. And though that's certainly valid for much of the magick we practice, think of the times you've practiced magick in a group. Certainly you know that working in a coven or circle or even attending a public ritual or a class once in a while (or, nowadays, practicing magick with a group online) has helped to not only amplify the power of the magick but also bring solidarity to the group. Certainly a family can do this, too. So here I've got a few suggestions for practicing magick with all members of the family.

Shielding

One of the most simple yet most important magickal tasks one can perform is shielding. Family members should shield themselves individually, but for scared or ill children of course Mom or Dad should do the shielding (or if you're sick, maybe Junior would like to do the honors). Remember that a feeling of safety and well-being should always be a part of magick, especially when children are involved.

The following technique is, I'm surprised to say, controversial. I've had people adamantly state that you cannot shield yourself before going to bed because you have to be awake to constantly send energy to the shields! This seems silly to me; after all, if you put barbed-wire fencing out to protect your business you don't need to stand there all night holding up the fence, now do you? In any case, I feel it is important for each person to shield him- or herself before going to sleep and also whenever it is thought to be needed, such as when scrying or before going into any stressful or possibly hazardous situation. So here's how it's done:

Sit or lie with eyes closed. Take a deep breath, and breathe slowly in and out, imagining breathing into each of the seven chakras, one at a time, starting with the root chakra. When the crown chakra is reached, breathe in and then, when exhaling, imagine a shower of sparks coming from the crown chakra as though a beautiful fireworks fountain, showering yourself with gleaming silver and gold sparks. Breathe in and out several times until you can see this image with the mind's eye. Then imagine these sparks forming a force field around yourself, sort of an electrified fence. This magickal force field will keep out intruders while allowing in positive attention.

Practice shielding before leaving for work or school in the morning and when going to bed at night. Do this as an exercise first before performing other kinds of magick or engaging in divination, and allow each person to modify the image of the shield any way he or she would like to imagine; sometimes mine comes out as a beautiful white and purple lotus flower or sometimes the fountain seems to have some amethyst crystals in it. Some folks like to see the "force field" as a column of pure white light or pink or blue or whatever color seems soothing and protective. (I wouldn't suggest red unless you're heavily into Set). Stephania Ebony suggests shielding your car or other transportation with a magickal "airplane skin" to protect it.

The Energy Beach Ball

If you practiced the energy raising exercise at the beginning of this chapter then you're ready to do this one. If not, go back and do it first. This activity is recommended for all ages, so when you're ready, get the family together and have everyone stand in a circle. First make sure that everyone *can* create energy between the palms of their hands. Have everyone do so individually.

Now, hold that energy between your hands as though you're holding a ball. Move your hands slowly apart, then move them around, encircling the energy until the "ball" is about the size of a basketball.

When everyone can accomplish this, we are ready to go on to the next step. Pair off facing each other. Merge your two basketballs of power until they are one. Each of you shares the holding of the ball, two hands on its sides, one below and one above. Now, slowly start moving your hands apart until you can create a ball of energy about the size of a beach ball (if you actually have a beach ball, you might try practicing with it first). See if each pair can keep the energy aloft by turning it every which way, or doing tricks amuses them. Talking and especially giggling while doing this exercise are not counterproductive and can even be encouraged!

When everyone is through with the exercise, gently lower arms to the sides and allow the energy to dissipate naturally. To hold onto some of the energy, place arms in front of your stomach with hands cupped, as if holding a ball against your abdomen. Breathe deeply and raise arms. Allow the reserved energy to wash over you, as though pouring a bowl of water over yourself. Lower arms and shake them out, then place palms on the floor to "ground" the energy. Try to practice this exercise at least once a week with the family, and as an individual, practice raising and controlling energy every day if possible. Now everyone in the family will be able to raise energy for spellwork when needed.

Scry Baby

It's been my experience that youngsters are drawn to divination but sometimes find the images on tarot cards to be rather frightening, and the same is true for some when in a darkened room with only a candle and crystal ball, scrying mirror, and so on. Learning methods of divination within the safety of the family can introduce this important skill while making it less intimidating. So here are a few techniques for "safe scrying."

1. If money's not an issue, take everyone in the family to a metaphysical bookstore or well-stocked chain bookstore and have each one pick out a tarot deck.

Make sure that each picks the deck he or she actually finds most appealing rather than picking the one that is the most expensive, most scary, and so on. Now each member of the family has his or her own deck to work with that should not be appropriated by other members of the family. After arriving home from the store, have each family member smudge his or her own deck with some incense on the altar or a sage or sweetgrass wand. This will "purify" the deck and consecrate it for use. You may want to have each person hold the deck while another smudges it, and all say, "I am pure; my tarot deck is pure," or something similar. After each has consecrated and shuffled his or her own deck, have each person pull a card. Look up the meaning of the card in a tarot text and discuss its possible relevance to the person who chose it. Do this once a day for a while until each person is comfortable with the deck and does not feel frightened by any of the seemingly negative images such as Death or the Devil.

2. If the family has one deck to use between them, let each family member shuffle the cards. Then the family should decide on a question to ask the cards. The most experienced diviner holds the cards while everyone focuses on the same question. Then one person draws a card from the deck (make sure that everyone gets a turn before the same person draws again). Look up the card's meaning, and discuss.

3. Encourage intuitive readings. Once a card is pulled, ask family members what they "see" in the card. Do any aspects of the illustrations see to leap off the page? What about personal symbolism? Flashes of intuition? Do not focus on which comments are "right" or "wrong" but rather see how these observations lead to greater awareness of the relationship between the literal meanings of the cards and their more personal and symbolic meanings.

4. With tarot cards, gradually work up to learning to do a full reading with whatever spread you wish. Usually the Celtic cross is used, but start off with something simpler, such as a three-card past, present, and future reading. Have books available that teach the philosophy of the tarot as "The Fool's Journey" and talk about the history of tarot as well as giving various spreads for various purposes.

5. If using a crystal ball or scrying mirror, darken the room somewhat but do not leave an inexperienced scryer alone. Ask the scryer to breathe deeply and slowly, relax, and try to focus on the scrying device. Start with five minutes per person and gradually work up to 15 minutes, but don't make anyone do this if he or she doesn't want to or feels that the exercise is non-productive. However, if participants want to give up right away it is a good idea to use this as a patience-training exercise and explain that images do not come easily and that only with practice and

patience will images appear. Smudge the scrying device before and after each person has used it.

6. If a particular family member feels drawn toward scrying but hasn't had luck seeing anything, then more training is needed. Ask the participant to hold a mental image of a particular object. Have him or her close his or her eyes and "see" the object in the mind's eye. Then have the person open his or her eyes and focus on the scrying device until he or she can "see" the object in the crystal. Believe me, it takes practice. I've been working with my crystal ball for about 30 years now and I still can't see a damn thing in it!

7. Let family members devise their own tarot or scrying exercises. If anyone still feels spooked by divination, make sure that the person can shield himself or herself before scrying.

Familiar Friends

Most youngsters (and quite a few of us oldsters, too) would love to have a familiar and thus start looking longingly at their pets. Well, before you go out and buy that miniature witch hat with the ear holes, read on. Sometimes a pet will want to be your familiar, and sometimes not. The best way to see if your companion animal wants to be your familiar is to take him or her into the magick circle with you and see how he or she reacts to ritual work or magick. Some animals will stand as if transfixed, and others will attempt to "help." Others, however, will do nothing but cause trouble during a ritual—knocking over the altar, jumping up on guests, making noise, and so forth. Still others will run like hell and hide under the bed at the first sign of a ritual knife. (Perhaps an unpleasant reminder of that "special" visit to the veterinarian.) In any case, explain to your children that pets are people, too, and that they have free will just as we human animals and therefore should not be forced into acting as a familiar if they don't want to. For all you know, your Scottie might be a Presbyterian or your French poodle an admirer of Voltaire and thus unlikely to attend any sort of religious rite.

But seriously, only allow animals into the magickal circle if they can behave themselves, and never leave an uncaged pet in a room alone with burning candles or incense!

Sometimes pets can act as familiars in other ways; many people have experienced the "laying on of paws" by their pets when the pet's human is ill. Sometimes pets seem to warn us of danger before it's coming, and we all know stories of animals saving their owners' lives. So just because your familiar won't help you call the corners doesn't mean that your pet is not in tune with the universe in another way.

And now, here's another type of familiar to entice into your life:

The Astral Familiar

I am not one to see ghosts or other phenomena, for that matter. Maybe that explains my strange reaction the day I met my astral familiar.

I have no pets because a) I am a cat person but am allergic to cats, and b) I'm not real fond of cleaning up after pets. Be that as it may, I did not seek out my astral familiar; he came looking for me.

My next-door neighbors had moved out a few weeks before it happened. One of their two cats, a gray-and-white-striped male, had disappeared as their goods were being moved from the apartment. They were very sad and I helped them look for the cat, which I had petted on many occasions. He didn't turn up, they moved out, and eventually I forgot about it.

But I think somehow that he didn't forget about *me*. One night I was coming home from teaching—cold-stone sober, mind you—at about 10 p.m. Walking up the short flight of brick stairs that lead to my townhouse, I was a few steps from my door when something streaked across the welcome mat before my door.

It was running, but its feet never touched the ground, and through its body I could clearly see the door and walls of the building. It was a gray-and-white-striped cat, and it vanished into the bushes.

Well. I stood there and I believe I said out loud, in pure Mr. Spock fashion, "Fascinating. I've just seen a ghost, and the ghost of a cat, at that." I didn't feel frightened and, oddly, the whole incident didn't really feel all that strange to me. I blinked my eyes a few times to make sure they weren't playing tricks on me. (Yes, I had my bifocals on!)

A friend suggested that I might have an astral familiar and that, because I'm allergic to living cats, I might as well cultivate the ghost cat as my familiar in an official capacity. To this day I do not know if the cat is the ghost of the cat that had lived next door, or if it only took that shape in order to appear familiar (ha, ha) to me.

I looked up some info on astral familiars and started reading *The Once Unknown Familiar* by Timothy Roderick to learn about my own relationship to "animal powers." While studying the book I remembered a bit of Russian folklore that suggests, when moving into a new place, leave the door open while bringing in the furniture and suchlike so that the *domovoy*, a domestic spirit, will take up residence. (I'm still trying figure out how to make the darned thing do dishes!) If a cat walks in, the domovoy will follow.

I did witness such an occurrence once. A friend of mine, coincidentally of Eastern European heritage, was moving into a new apartment after the passing of his mother. As I walked into his new place while he was still moving boxes in, a black cat followed me inside. I told him the story of the domovoy and he seemed to feel that perhaps it was possible. He petted the cat and immediately took a liking to it. As it turns out the cat belonged to the apartment complex as a sort of shared pet; it apparently was part of the welcoming committee as well. Later on he told me that at the time he had felt that the cat was an emissary of his deceased mother, but that he had been too embarrassed to admit it right then.

So I decided that I would try for a relationship with the ghost cat as my astral familiar. I left milk outside at night; I called to it; and I have seen it a few times since then, oddly enough, manifesting in different colors and sizes, the most recent being that of an orange tabby or what the British call a marmalade cat. I believe that all these manifestations are of the same spirit, perhaps appearing in various guises depending on what "cat suit" he or she wants to wear at the time!

I talk to my astral familiar and ask for its blessings. I've seen it at the foot of my bed acting as a "watchcat." I've considered meeting it on its own level during astral travel.

Others who are sensitive to such things have said that they felt the presence of the astral cat. I'm perfectly happy with it so far. Just so long as it doesn't ask me to clean its astral litter box....

If you cannot have a pet for whatever reason you might try to attract an astral familiar. You can certainly try the moving-in exercise and see if a real cat turns up; remember, it's ushering in a benevolent house spirit, so be sure you want that as well. You might try to contact an astral familiar by "conjuring" one, and the easiest way to do that is through guided imagery, or guided visualization.

Follow the visualization here. I've used variations on it for many purposes, including leading creative writing students to their muses. People seem to get a lot out of it, so why not try it to find your astral familiar?

Meeting Your Astral Familiar

Sit or lie comfortably, but not so comfortably that you will fall asleep. You may wish to cast a circle before you begin the meditation. Ground and run energy. Then close your eyes, and take three deep breaths, inhaling through your nose and exhaling through your mouth in pranic breathing fashion.

Visualize yourself in a public building, such as a museum or library. Take note of your surroundings; they will give you valuable clues to the nature of your relationship with the astral familiar.

Orient yourself inside, and then walk toward the door of the building that leads outside. When you exit, you will see that there are 10 steps down to the sidewalk. Across the sidewalk you see a large park. Now have someone count down for you from 10 to 1, or record the steps yourself. Get deeper into the meditation with each step.

Once you are outside, look at the park. What is it like? Who populates it? Are there children playing, families picnicking, joggers or athletes exercising or playing a game? Become comfortable with the park.

Now look from side to side. You will see a park bench a little way up the sidewalk. Which way will you walk to the bench, to the right or left? Take note of this.

Feel the elements all around you: the warmth of the sun, the scent of the air, the feel of the ground beneath your feet, a cool mist on the breeze. Which element symbolizes the familiar you would like to meet?

Walk around a bit to orient yourself and experience the four elements in sacred space. Now approach the bench. Sit down on it and enjoy the park. Try to hear any human and animal sounds around yourself.

Look into the distance. After a few moments you should see a figure, far away, beginning to approach. As the figure approaches, note its shape. It gradually comes into view; what type of animal is it? Take some time to allow it to approach. If you feel afraid at any time or feel that this is not the right time to be doing this visualization or that this is not the right animal to be your familiar, just take three deep breaths and open your eyes into the here and now. But if you wish to continue, allow the animal to approach, and greet it appropriately; for example, if it is a cat you may stroke its head; if it is a dog you may wish to "shake hands" with it, and so forth.

What does the animal do? How does it react to your presence and your touch? If the reaction is positive and you feel that this is the right animal, then ask it to be your familiar. Does it indicate that it wants to be your familiar? If so, then you may wish to spend some quality time with it before ending the meditation.

When you are ready to say "ta-ta-for-now" to your new astral friend and soon-to-be familiar, say good-bye and get up off the bench. Walk toward the building. When you get to the stairs, ascend one at a time while someone counts from one to 10. When you reach the top of the stairs, open your eyes. If you have met your familiar, now is the time to think about how you will work with it and what you will expect from the relationship. If not, then you might want to work with the meditation more until you feel you have met the right entity. I also suggest reading the previously mentioned *The Once Unknown Familiar* for an in-depth way to work with animal powers.

Well, because we're talking about family, I might as well conclude with a family tale of my own. My family dwindles every year; I am an only child and many of my cousins have chosen, as I have, to remain childless. So the opportunities for "family magick" are scarce indeed. Oh, of course I've acted as foster grandmother (that's punk-rock grandma to you, bud!) at magickal gatherings where there were kids and pets; in fact, I sort of prefer hanging out with the kids and pets—no need to compete with other grown-ups about silly things such as who's sexiest or richest or the most accomplished mage. So in that sense, yes, I've practiced with families, and we welcome families in our Iseum. But what about my actual, real family? Well, let me tell you my story:

She Always Made Do

My uncle Forrest was a well-known lawyer, partied with the politicos here in California, and knew all those famous lawyers you see on TV. So why would he tell people that he admired my grandmother, Florence, who scraped along on her late husband's minuscule pension and a little bit of Social Security?

Because she "always made do," he said. He felt that she was a genius at getting along on practically nothing. And if that's not magick, then I don't know what is.

Grandmother Florence, whom I called Grammie, was always babysitter to my best friend and me. She was the best babysitter ever: She'd let us eat popcorn, ice cream, and Cokes for supper, if that's what we wanted; she'd play school with us or any board game you could think of, and we could watch all the TV we wanted! (She didn't like horror movies, however; they seemed a little too real to her. I especially remember her fear of the movie *Them*, one of those 1950s big bug movies in which giant ants parade through the flood channels of L.A. That scared the bejesus out of her.) I'm not sure my parents knew about any of this, but I figure what they didn't know in this case didn't hurt them any!

It was from her that my dad got his famous psychic streak and probably where I got some of my mojo, too, though I also thank my maternal grandfather for some of that. But what made me think of her recently was a typical Hollywood moment on TV.

It was during the Academy Awards when Jamie Foxx got up to accept his Oscar. He thanked his grandmother for always setting him on the right course and said that, now that she has passed on,

"She only speaks to me in my dreams."

I burst out crying at that point, because I think I knew exactly how he feels (he was crying at this point as well). Grammie has indeed visited me in my dreams, and I've felt her watching over me—usually sitting on the edge of the bed with her hair in a bun and, wearing over a housedress, one of those crocheted cardigan sweaters she liked.

So that's my sappy "family magick" story. There are more, but we'll save them for another time when they might be more appropriate.

And now, for a humorous interlude:

The Full Moon Familiar Follies

Here's what happens when two witless witches incorporate animals into their full moon rituals without really thinking things through.

The full moon was in Taurus on the Tuesday night previous to the time in which I'm writing this piece. Well, I have the moon in Taurus in my astrological chart, so after work I thought I'd do a little impromptu full moon ritual. It was beautiful outside, a perfect global-warming evening, 75 degrees in November! Out on the balcony I caught reflections of moonlight in the spring water in the sacred chalice that I'd never managed to do as successfully ever before! I was thrilled.

As this was a spur-of-the-moment ritual I pulled some stuff together: statues of Isis and Horus, spring water, white candles, and some essential oils in a diffuser. I called on the four sons of

Horus—Duamatef, Quebsenuf, Imsety, and Hapi—and cast a circle. I had a few reasons to pour my heart out to Isis and so I did. All this was taking place in my all-purpose home-office-and-temple and I was sitting in one of my typing chairs before the altar. After I had gotten a little weepy, I leaned forward in the chair a bit, and then I heard a loud MEEOOWWW.

Ahem. I had no idea what to think. At first I thought it was the chair, so I leaned back, leaned forward, sideways, swiveled around in it, but couldn't make it even squeak, much less make any sound that even vaguely resembled meow.

Then I jumped up and said, "Bast, is that you? Bastet? Are you there?" I dashed around the room looking for—what? I have no idea. And I immediately felt foolish. It must be my astral familiar, of course! I rushed around the room looking for a sign of the cat. I didn't see anything, but I darn sure heard that meow. I felt very happy; my astral familiar was back! And after all that calling out to Bast, I named my astral familiar Basteycat. Not very creative, but it sounds a little bit arty, maybe as someone with dyslexia would try to say the name of the artist "Basquiat." I welcomed back my familiar and when I went to bed I asked him (her?) to be my guardian.

Meanwhile, unbeknownst to me, across town, my own co-writer Lori Nyx had decided to do a spur-of-the-moment full moon ritual herself. At the same time as I was doing my ritual, she was petsitting at Barney's house; Barney is the large black Newfoundland that she takes care of when his owner is away; she mentioned him in her chapter on Anubis in *The Dark Archetype*. Anyway, she left him in the house and went outside with her impromptu tools—in her case, a candle, a bottle of ale with a picture of a demon on it (well, this is Nyx we're talking about), and a gingerbread boy—and proceeded to set up for the ritual and spellwork.

Well, Barney whined and begged at the back door and wanted to join her so she let him out. He immediately tried to eat the gingerbread boy and drink the ale, but she persuaded him to stay across the yard and behave. Right in the middle of her ritual, he decided it was time to use the bathroom, and—well, let's just say that the moon was in Taurus, but that was no load of B.S. Lori told me that she thought it might have been a commentary on her spell from the cosmos. After his *toilette* Barney acted very happy and, because the spell was broken anyway, he finally got to eat the by-this-time ale-soaked gingerbread boy.

So much for pets and rituals and the witches that think they're in control of the situation. So did my astral familiar really manifest or am I just crazy? Wait, don't answer that.

The Grimoire and Your Magickal Scrapbook

Does anyone still keep a grimoire, that "book of shadows" that records spells, rituals, prayers, and the results of same? I've heard that some witches now keep theirs as a blog on the Internet! That seems a bit too public for me; remember that originally grimoires were only to be shared with one's coven or circle, if shared at all; often they were kept completely confidential, a relationship between practitioner and grimoire only.

With so much information available in books, in magazines, and on the Internet, it seems a bit redundant these days to keep one's own grimoire. Yes, it is important to keep notes on your progress and note other things such as the when and where and the outcomes of spells and rituals you've done. And yes, I have a lovely grimoire with a picture of Thoth on the cover. It's still blank, I'm ashamed to say. Why? Well, it's easier to keep spells, rituals, and whatnot in files on my computer and on backup disks. I also annotate the books I use, so my marginal notes are there the next time I use something from that book.

Clearly, keeping a handwritten grimoire seems a bit quaint and old-fashioned. Some of us just don't have time to write things out by hand. (And some of us can't read our own handwriting.) My point is that other means are available, so all those Word files of spells and rituals really do constitute a 21st-century grimoire. If you also wish to keep one the old-fashioned way, that's great. But don't feel guilty if you don't do so.

On the other hand, here is a magickal exercise that the Iseum of Isis Paedusis gives to its members:

The Magickal Scrapbook

When proceeding on a path towards initiation, which, as DeTraci Regula does, I feel is a lifelong process, it's important to keep that process in mind. In our Iseum's case this means that we assign a scrapbooking exercise to all of our members.

Yes, scrapbooking. I didn't even know that was a real word until one of my composition students wrote a paper about it!

It seems to be a popular hobby these days, and here is how it fits in with this exercise:

I will use the example of how we use it in the Iseum and anyone can adapt it to make it more relevant to his or her own path. First, buy any type of scrapbook you find appealing. We tell our dedicants (our members are dedicated to one or more Egyptian deities) to watch the media for info on Egypt such as TV shows, magazine and Internet articles, films, art exhibits, plays, and so on. In fact, it seems as if almost any night of the week there is something about Egypt on one of the cable channels. The dedicant is expected to cut out the article or listing and paste it in the scrapbook and to watch the programs whenever possible and take notes. The notes can be typed and pasted into the scrapbook as well. The purpose of the exercise is to learn as much as possible about ancient Egypt and its daily life, beliefs, deities, art, culture, and so forth. Thus the magickal scrapbook provides easy access to information that is not otherwise conveniently located in a book.

Keeping the magickal scrapbook is another way to be mindful of one's path while enjoying it more. My example can be easily adapted: Though Egypt is a popular topic for pop media, there are others as well; surely there are as many cable TV specials about Stonehenge, the Vikings, and ancient Greece and Rome as there are about King Tut!

Attending a lecture, art exhibit, or play is another way to experience one's path. Put the playbill or any other printed info you receive in the scrapbook. Postcards or other pictures of ancient art seen in museums (some museums do allow photography, but not all) in person should go into the scrapbook as well. Just glancing through your scrapbook will then remind you of what you saw, experienced, and learned.

And hey, if you want to get really into it, why not take one of those popular scrapbooking courses that are taught at various arts and crafts stores and community education programs? Then when someone in the course says, "Would you like to see some pictures of my grandchildren?" You can always reply with, "Sure. Wanna see a picture of my mummy?"

Love Magick

I am not the right person to be writing about this! As Stephania Ebony says, it is a topic best left untouched sometimes, no pun intended. First let's talk about love magick for couples, and then for those who, for want of a better word, are un-coupled.

Couples magick goes into the arena of sex magick in many cases. Sex magick is not without its dangers; for one thing, if you perform it with a person who is not suitable for you in the first place, then you have just forged a very strong bond with someone you may end up not wanting to be involved with at all. Sex magick should also not be attempted as a selfish act—that is, if one person wants to use the energy created during sex to accomplish his or her own magickal goal without the other person benefiting from or knowing about it. Also, because it is possible (and even likely) that one person in a couple may be of our magickal ilk and the other not of our faith, then it would be wrong to coerce that person or put the guilt trip or him or her for not wanting to participate.

There are a lot of sex magick books out there, some of them fairly sleazy. (No, really?) There is, however, one that I would unequivocally recommend: Selene Silverwind's *Magic for Lovers: Create Lasting Love with Wicca Spells and Tantric Techniques*. This is a lovely, very erotic book with explicit instructions. I envy those couples who decide to try her methods!

If you are part of a couple whether or not you wish to perform sex magick there are methods of keeping your love life fresh and alive. I can recommend *Enchantments of the Heart* by Dorothy Morrison, a book about love magick that helps keep lovers in love. There are some delightful and I daresay some darned practical yet romantic suggestions in this book. Probably the best way to magickally maintain a love relationship on a daily basis is the same as doing so non-magickally, for really, isn't all love magick? Simply do this: Don't take your partner for granted. Interpret this anyway you wish, and act on it according to your own taste. Some women do love it when their husbands bring them one perfect rose every day; others, as Dorothy Parker reminds us, wonder why he never gives them "one perfect Cadillac."

Just when I think I have a handle on all this love stuff, what should come my way? Another delightful reason to display my font of knowledge, this time about a particular type of love:

"Poly" Want a Cracker?

There seems to be a new movement going on in the complex world of relationships these days—it's called "polyamory." It feels to me that every time I turn a corner at a Renaissance Faire, science fiction convention, or pagan faire or gathering, there's a group of people bound and determined (no, I refuse to talk about B&D! Get your mind out of the gutter!) to tell us all about the wonderful new thing they've discovered for the very first time ever: polyamory, the practice of committing oneself to more than one love partner.

Back in the 70s in the suburbs, didn't they used to call that "wife swapping"? (How come it was never called "husband swapping"?) Well, some of these poly people took umbrage at that comment and explained to me that they weren't just sleeping around but were in fact committed to more than one person. Holy cats, I was at Loscon, the Los Angeles Science Fantasy Society's annual convention, and evidently a whole group of these people had a handfasting there.

Group is the operative word here, as in the past this practice was in fact called "group marriage." It came out of the 60s with a variety of other counter-cultural ideas, but even then it wasn't new. Utopian groups in the past had tried it on for size, with the practice going back centuries. Sorry, kids, you didn't invent the idea.

Now, I can't say I can address this issue objectively, being the old crank that I am. I mean, I was married for more than a decade (I think that's a record in Los Angeles County) and I can tell you that being married to just one person is hard enough. The idea of sharing my life with more than one person just sort of gives me indigestion.

At a ritual recently I met a young man who says he is polyamorous but who was very concerned because he feels he is growing apart from his wife. I wonder what happens if they do get a divorce; who gets custody of the other people in the relationship?

So boldly go where, in reality, many have gone before. Francisco Arcaute calls me the last Victorian writer, so in closing I'll just repeat what was said in the Victorian era about certain sexual practices:

"I don't care what you do as long as long as you don't do it out in the street and frighten the horses."

So when I speak of everyday love magick I will take a different tack, and take my cues from different sources: the chakra system and feng shui.

Most pagans know about the chakras, at least the seven main ones, and I will follow this discussion with the means for learning about them and keeping them healthy. In truth there are many more than just those seven; there are at least 21 more minor charkas, according to Dr. Brenda Davies, author of *The 7 Healing Chakras* and *Unlocking the Heart Chakra*. Most of us know that we need to clear our chakras every so often; I tend to imagine them as spark plugs that can get gunked up and then misfire, but then I'm a product of California car culture. Clearing the chakras so that they move smoothly as though nice deosil whirlpools is the idea. But healing the heart chakra is a special situation: To heal your relationship with love, you have to really work with this one.

Chakras that are muddy with stagnant energy and little movement are called "blocked" or "locked" chakras. Clearly when we have been hurt in love relationships we have a "broken heart" and we may want to either consciously or unconsciously "lock up" that heart chakra and throw away the key so that it doesn't happen again. And that's understandable. But clogging up the system by blocking the central chakra—there are three main ones below it and three main ones above—is a really bad idea healthwise. So start working on that heart chakra. Keeping it open and clear keeps you open to love in all its forms and also projects a message of love from you to the outside world that makes everyone think more kindly of you. People whose hearts are "broken" often seem mad at the world and others may not want to be around them; even if you do not want to start a new love relationship I don't think you really want to completely shut down love in your life, or you would be rejecting the love and kindness of friends, family, and colleagues, not to mention the love of the deities and the "universe" in general. People who've given up on love and have shut down their heart chakras often seem to be black holes: Direct at them any sort of kindness, overtures of friendship, or even a simple compliment, and you risk being pulled into the vortex of their bitterness and anger.

"Hey, Susie, what a great dress!"

"This old thing? It makes me look fat."

&

"Jerry! The boys are having a little get-together on Friday to play Texas Hold 'Em. You in?"

"Now why would I want to spend time with those losers?"

These exchanges are pretty close to real situations I've encountered with people who have shut down their heart chakras. Those people seem to be living a self-fulfilling prophecy: Act that way toward others and, sure enough, after a while nobody will like them or even want to come near them.

Usually, when there is a problem with the heart chakra, there is also a problem with the main chakra below the heart and the one above. The one below is the solar plexus chakra. When you visualize it, does the lovely sunny yellow it should be get mixed up with icky bile green? If so, then there's a problem. Similarly, look to your throat chakra, the chakra of communication. Is it a clear bright blue or is it an ugly, muddy dark blue, as though someone had thrown a bucket of gray paint into it?

The heart chakra itself should be a pure emerald green. Some people like to visualize it as pink, because they like to use rose quartz for love, but this is not traditional, and I prefer the traditional way. Buy a box of the Chanakara melon green tea, which is Chanakara's tea for the heart chakra and have a cup each day until you feel better about things and your heart chakra clears up. Then buy a box of the Chanakara selected teas for all the chakras and try them too around the time of month you decide to clear your charkas. (You should do so at least that often, if not more.) I'll speak about dealing with all the chakras a bit later.

Remember that love begins with loving yourself. If you can drink that Chanakara melon green tea while feeling positive about yourself, you have just done a very subtle little love spell that will eventually, through practice, bring you back into the fold of the universe's (and everyone else's) loving energy.

Another method for creating and maintaining love in your life is feng shui. You can always hire a feng shui specialist to "do" your house if you can afford it; this is, of course, quite expensive—and reasonably so, for feng shui is a very complex study that should not be oversimplified, and folks who are experts in it have studied *a lot*. Beware of books on the subject that oversimplify it.

My favorite book on feng shui is called *Move Your Stuff, Change Your Life* by Karen Rauch Carter. It is written (obviously!) for Westerners in a fun, colloquial manner while still maintaining the rigor of feng shui and being honest about it with the casual reader. I go by some of her simpler suggestions, and she does have quite a few that don't require heavy-duty restructuring of your abode and its furnishings.

To bring and keep love in your life, work on the bedroom. Keep it dusted and vacuumed. The best colors, of course, are red, pink, and white. I try to keep to this color scheme; my bedroom furniture is white and I have cranberry glass collectibles in a hutch atop the larger chest of drawers. The bedspread, curtains, and other furnishings are in shades of burgundy. There is Egyptian artwork on the walls and the bedspread has a Middle-Eastern-like pattern. I had originally meant it to look perhaps similar to Cleopatra's boudoir, but considering my lack of decorating prowess it sort of turned out to be what I now call Early Moroccan Bordello—but that's okay; you should know that you pretty much have to have a sense of humor if you're gonna hang around with me.

I do have pink and red candles around the room and now have a small altar to Oshun, the *orisha* of love, often called the African Venus. I spritz Bulgarian rose hydrosol around the room and have rose potpourri, too. I keep my lotions and perfumes in the bedroom as they are symbols of sensuality.

Designing a room to attract and keep love need not be overtly sexual; remember that love is comprised of many facets. Comfort, friendship, peace, joy, and intimacy are also part of it, so there should be no unhappy faces or bouquets of dead roses—as much as I love dead roses, and I do—in this room. I also keep electronics out of the bedroom; electromagnetic radiation is *not* good for you, especially when you sleep. If you have a TV, computer, or other outputter of large amounts of electromagnetic radiation then I strongly suggest you move them to another room. Why are you watching TV in bed, anyway? Shouldn't you have something better to do there? Just a thought.

I remember a story Carter told in *Move Your Stuff* about a woman who wondered why she was still single when she felt she had done everything in her power to attract a man, including using the right kind of feng shui—or so she thought. The author looked around the woman's bedroom. She found that the only pictures in the bedroom were of the woman herself, alone, and pictures of other single people. When she moved some of these pictures and instead put in pictures of couples, she quickly met someone appropriate and was soon involved in a successful relationship.

Other suggestions involve keeping fresh flowers or, better yet, a living plant in the bedroom. Living things and things that move are all attractors of positive *chi*, according to the feng shui experts. Placing a musical instrument in the room—for an Isian, perhaps a sistrum—or the traditional wooden flute is suggested. Make sure the room gets light and air, and don't sleep with your feet facing the door if at all possible. Move old stuff, such as any reminders of unhappy times and/or past relationships, out of the room.

Keeping your bedroom a comfortable, loving, and attractive space will help get and keep that significant other. But there are other ways. My film industry friend Jeff Helgason, a Reiki practitioner, told me another simple feng shui trick: Buy a pair of ceramic ducks, such as a set of salt and pepper shakers, and keep them in the kitchen on or near the stove. Apparently, ducks mate for life and the heat of the stove symbolizes passion. Try it if you desire a passionate, long-term relationship.

Once you've feng shui-ed the place, you don't need to maintain it on a daily basis; just make sure it's clean, remove any dead plants or flowers, and empty the wastebasket frequently.

These methods approach love as a way to be open to possibilities and to foster and maintain love in a non-manipulative manner. Most love spells are considered too manipulative to be ethical and keeping up the appearance of a sex-bomb is just too tiring to do 24/7. And if you're honest and open to love, you shouldn't have to anyway.

While we're on the topic, why not a prayer for love? Some of us may feel we need more than a prayer, but oh well, here goes....

Love Victorious

Throwing off old chains
And tired notions,
I accept the universe as Love
And know that I deserve
The kindness, the friendship,
And yes, the love
Of deity, of the universe,
Of those who would walk with me
Throughout my life.
I open myself to love
And welcome in
Those who would share with me
In perfect love,
And perfect trust,

That same walk through life
In whatever form
Is meant to be.

Okay, do we need some love affirmations, too? Well, that poem was sort of a loooong affirmation, so here's a couple of simpler ones that would lend themselves to memorization more easily:

Love is my state of being

Kindness and love surround me

And don't forget this all-important one:

I am beautiful and loved.

Say it and make it so! Okay, here's where I get to impress the Trekkers: Captain Picard is famous for saying "make it so," a sort of version of "so mote it be." Well, now my ancestral French home is in Normandy, but when my ancestors lived there the county lines were drawn differently, and it was in Picardy. So I am a real Picardian. Take that, *Star Trek* fans!

I couldn't bear to end the section on love magick without adding a few words about what could go wrong in our fabulous world of relationships. Men and women who are in the Craft have a tendency to trust others of their faith a little too much right away; oftentimes, especially if you live in an area where few people are "out of the broom closet," just meeting someone who shares your beliefs might be enough to make you fall head over heels. Strive to keep your head where it belongs: squarely on your shoulders. Yes, it would be nice to think that we're all brothers and sisters and always treat each other well. It would be nice…sorry it ain't always so, however. Keep your wits about you. That guy dressed as if he's part of Wolf Clan might really be a wolf of another kind.

Clearing and Balancing the Chakras

Some people do this every month or every week; some, including the author of *The 7 Healing Chakras*, do it every day in the shower. I prefer to clear the chakras while lying down and comfortable, just before shielding and going to sleep.

For some this will be a review and for others it may be totally new, as the chakra system comes from Eastern beliefs—as does feng shui—and so it may not be familiar to all pagans. But Wiccans and pagans are greatly ecumenical—we find what works and then we use it!

Think of the chakras as whirling balls of light. That little whirly thing on the computer that tells you the computer is trying to do something is a good example. Each of the chakras is a different color. I recommend clearing and balancing the chakras as a daily activity if you are going through a big event in your life such as the loss of a loved one, losing or obtaining a job, or having gone through a natural disaster, such as the recent hurricanes. The break-up of a relationship, the completion of a big business deal, attending an event where there are lots and lots of people, graduating from school—all sorts of activities both positive and negative can tax your chakras. Some of your chakras, such as the heart chakra mentioned previously, may need extra attention on a continuing basis, especially if you have been a victim of abuse or have suffered the loss of many loved ones in your life so far, especially parents or spouses. Generally speaking, you plan to clear your chakras once a week.

Some people speak in terms of "opening" and "closing" the chakras. I think it's more important to keep them healthy and alive as a channel for *chi*, rather than worrying about opening them to a universe that might not always be that benevolent, or closing them off to the opportunities out there. So for me, balance is the right word. Keep them clear and clean, and you've done your job.

To clear the chakras, start at the bottom and work up. Here they are:

1. The root chakra. Visualize this as a wheel of red light, located near the base of your spine and radiating throughout your hips, the eliminative system, and the external genitals. Some people like to believe that all the sex organs belong to the next chakra, but I say they're just being a tad squeamish about all that blatant red energy.

2. The second chakra, the sacral chakra, is seen as a wheel of orange light, somewhere between the shades of orange juice and carrot juice. It fills the lower digestive system and the internal sex organs. Trying to reconcile this chakra with the root chakra should be a goal.

3. The third chakra is the solar plexus chakra. It is a sunny yellow. It is very important for it reigns over many vital organs, such as the stomach, liver, pancreas, spleen, and so on. When you "vent your spleen," as expressing anger has been called, you are said to have "blown" this chakra. Hmm. No wonder I have trouble with this chakra. You will need to spend extra time healing if this is the case.

4. The fourth chakra is the heart chakra, the very center of one's being. This chakra is bright sparkling green like an emerald. It rules not only the heart and the circulatory system but also the arms, hands, and upper torso. Most of us tend to have problems with this chakra from time to time. Remember that the number one killer of both men and women in the United States continues to be heart disease. Try to put more "ease" into your heart chakra.

5. The throat chakra is the one I'm maxing out right now trying to write this book. It rules communication our "voice," our neck, throat, and the blood vessels leading to and coming from the brain. It is a rich blue, not teal or turquoise, but not navy blue, either. It might be considered royal blue or ultramarine.

6. The "third eye" chakra is located mid-forehead just above and between the eyes in the location of the pineal gland, and unfortunately I can't get the image of Jeff Combs in *From Beyond* and his prodigious pineal gland out of my mind when I talk about it.

Sorry; movies are my life sometimes. It rules our organs of perception and all parts of the brain not ruled by the throat or crown chakra. It is indigo. Did you know that the only animal left with an actual "third eye" is the tuatara, a primitive lizard that lives in New Zealand?

7. The crown chakra is the last; some say it is above the top of the head, floating in space. It is either amethystine purple or clear, as a quartz crystal is. This chakra rules our higher intellectual and spiritual functions. It is our pathway to the cosmos.

To begin, lie or sit down so that you are comfortable—no uncomfortable meditation postures, although the chakras are often depicted on someone sitting in the lotus position. I feel that comfort is necessary when concentrating on specific parts of the body.

Visualize a red wheel of light in the area of your tailbone. See it begin to whirl deosil (clockwise). Look for imperfections, such as dark or unclear spots in the color, or if the color itself is "off." Just observe to start with, then go on to the next one and continue up.

When you have reached the crown chakra, you may see it the way you feel comfortable: to look at it as open to the cosmos may feel too revealing; you can look at it as something of a halo if you wish, instead! In fact, it has been suggested that the haloes seen in paintings of holy men and women are meant to show this very chakra as a symbol of their purity.

Once you've got the chakras spinning nicely, you can shield yourself, and drift off to sleep. Deal with imperfections in the colors of the chakras next time you try this, for it takes practice. If you feel seriously out of whack then see a professional who can clear your chakras for you; many magickal practitioners and bodyworkers can do this for a fee.

It's well worth it to learn to clear and balance your own chakras. Don't expect, however, for them to ever be as perfect as the pictures in books. We can only work toward perfection, knowing that its actual attainment is merely a guideline, never a requirement.

Finding Your Magickal Talents

Well, I've talked about a lot of magickal tasks here and a few talents, perhaps. What about others? I've learned that I'm pretty hopeless with the crystal ball and that my effect on living plants is something worthy of Morticia Adams. So, okay, those aren't my strong suits; but did I tell you I can do psychometry? And did I mention that I wish I couldn't?

Yeah, my friends love to tell me of the great bargains they get at resale clothing shops. But I can't join them in their fun; you see, I am a bit of a natural psychometrist, and that means that I can sense the presence, others through their clothing, jewelry, and so forth. Secondhand clothes carry "vibes," as I'll call them. I wish it weren't so; I'd have more options when it came to shopping. But that's the way it is, for me, anyway.

Is psychometry something you want to explore? What about clairvoyance, or clairaudience? Maybe you'd like to try your luck with the Ouija board, or pratice your astral projection. These are all fun talents that can be cultivated. You'll be better at some than at others, and some you'll just want to abandon altogether. But start by informing yourself. Read some books; attend some classes at local New Age or Wiccan bookstores. I'm sure there are Yahoo groups or other online groups out there on these topics that you could join. My point is, experiment! Have fun! Isn't that what it's all about? I mean, magick may be a responsibility, but it shouldn't be a chore. It should be a lifelong pursuit requiring study and practice, and, trust me, if you keep learning it never gets boring. If it did, believe me, after all these years I wouldn't bother with it!

So vary your magickal pursuits and magickal tasks. Work with what works for you now; that may change later on. Explore different cultures and practices; we here in America are the luckiest people on earth for we are exposed to virtually every type of person and culture on earth right here at home. My favorite thing to do is visit ethnic neighborhoods and learn about their foods, their culture, their customs, their magick. I hope you will, too. Go outside your comfort zone. It's the only way to really grow.

It's an almost-full moon tonight and, wow, if that's not magick all by itself, then I don't know what is.

Chapter 8

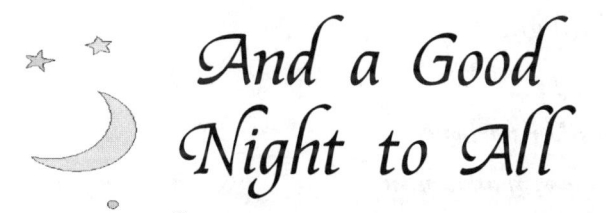

And a Good Night to All

Affirmations

*May Anubis guard me while I sleep
And his blessed mother Nephthys
Watch over my dreams.*

※

I await Morpheus, and welcome his presence.

※

*May black Isis draw her veil around me
And bring me soothing sleep.*

May the Sandman be mindful of my optometry bill.
Doh! Just funnin' with ya. I promise to be good now.

A Prayer

Lady of Twilight

Lady of Twilight
Traveler of silver starlight
Pull your cloak around the sun
And softly dim the lights
To amber gloaming.
Lady of Twilight
Traveler of silver starlight
Bless the evening of my day
With your tender initiation
Of dusk, that lustrous between-time
Introducing evening
To day.

Some magicians love twilight. They feel that it is the natural time of day when the veil between the world becomes translucent; a great calm descends on the worlds, and each side can glimpse the other. When my day turns to evening, I often think of the fog that starts to roll in at dusk where I live as a cloud-soft pashmina shawl, dimming the day's brightness with a cool, muffled cloud. Though the evening cloud cover often obscures the sunset, it is in itself a kind of "sun-setting" spectacle.

And no one can deny the spectacle of a good sunset; long considered the most romantic time of day, how often do lovers jockey for the best seats in the best restaurants at sunset! If modern man ever is aware of his natural surroundings during the day, it is at sunset. Perhaps that's another reason why it's a magickal time of day. Everyone focusing on it and putting their own spin on its significance, whether romantic or otherwise, certainly generates a great deal of energy. Some people love sunsets for their beauty alone; it is ironic that the smog that infests so many of our cities also makes their sunsets more colorful and dramatic.

Twilight, on the other hand, was not seen as a positive time by the Vikings. The rune assigned to symbolize twilight was Dagaz, the rune for day, but also the rune of Loki, the trickster god. It is a term used ominously in the phrase *Twilight of the Gods*, or *Ragnarok*, the battle that initiates the end of the world as we know it. If you wish to think of this time of day as dangerous, then abstain from magick during this time. Twilight is, by the way, the most dangerous time of the day to drive, and coincidentally—at least when it's not daylight savings time—rush hour! When the world is neither fully light nor fully dark our senses don't quite know what to make of it; be very, very careful when driving or crossing streets while walking at this time of day.

As sunset moves us toward twilight we can think of this magickal time as a time to walk between the worlds and do whatever kind of magick we would normally do there. Ever notice how all the cats in the neighborhood come out and sit on the front lawns at twilight? Hmmm. We really need not wait until Samhain to walk between the worlds; we have a chance to do so once a day, every day.

People who consider themselves "morning people" feel the pull of the sunset more dramatically than night owls such as myself. For them, the setting sun seems to cast a spell that whispers to them, "Night is coming; it's bedtime, time to go to sleep" and I've heard many a morning person speak of how hard it is to stay up in the evening once they have observed the sunset.

It's a shame that in our heavily regulated society we usually can't decide the hours we wish to keep; a "morning person" should be able to awake before dawn and go to sleep when night falls if he or she wishes; the "night person" should be able to sleep until 9 a.m. and stay up late. Rarely do we have such a luxury.

This is one reason why our society runs on chronic sleep deprivation; one reason why there's a Starbucks on every corner; and one reason why toxic stress is a part of most peoples' lives. We are forcefully disconnected from our own biorhythms by the dictates of our schedules, artificially enforced by the structured regimen of our society. This disconnection with nature results in many of us feeling disoriented much of the time.

Evening should be for repose. It should be family time—time to relax, relate, and discuss the events of the day. As it is, many of us work in the evenings, or attend school, and rarely get to see our friends and families during this traditional "downtime."

I remember with great joy those summer vacations of my childhood when my dad would work swing shift (it was beastly hot in the Northrop plant during the day in summertime). I got to play outside until it got dark and then could stay up watching "grown-up" TV such as *One Step Beyond* and *Burke's Law* while waiting for my dad to get home at midnight. I remember the scent of the night-blooming jasmine and the fragrant datura flowers called "angel trumpets" that grew in the front yard. My mom has always said I am a night person; she thinks this is because I was born around two in the afternoon and that somehow set my biorhythm to be most "awake" later in the day. Starting school again in the fall meant more grueling early mornings of dragging myself out of bed so as not to be late for class.

This year I had to teach on Halloween evening. You can imagine how unhappy I was about that; my students were, too. So I arranged something special for them: I had two wonderful poets, Dr. Richard Jennings and Michelle Mitchell-Foust, come to each of my classes and read horror and supernatural poetry and discuss the lure of all the "scary" stuff we love at Halloween. An animated conversation took place; people who had never spoken in class before related their own ghost stories and brought up other such "forbidden" topics. As darkness settled around us, the dimly lit English department lounge where we held the readings became a place outside of time for that evening, a place of mystery and wonder.

If only every night could be that way! I am well aware of the dangers of working at night; besides the obvious ones, scientists have found that there is a link between breast cancer and women who work at night. Apparently, this "unnatural" cycle disrupts the body's immune system, allowing cancer cells to get a toehold in one's system. A very scary thought that is, indeed; I wonder what else we are doing to ourselves by working after dark.

So for the sake of our health—both physical and spiritual—let's try to keep some of the evening as a magickal time. Marking the sunset is one such activity. If you can stop what you're doing for even a moment at sunset and observe the way one half of the day separates from the other you are doing good for yourself. On days when the sunset hours are your own, try some sunset magick.

Sunset and Vines

If you can connect with nature during the sunset then you have an ideal situation for casting a spell. This is especially recommended on the solstices and equinoxes. Our Iseum's Mabon ritual took place at a public park at sunset on the first day of fall; we faced west toward the altar and so we faced the setting sun while doing our ritual, a very beneficent arrangement all the way around. We made sure that autumn leaves, fallen berries, and other natural items we picked up in the park were used as decorations along with the store-bought variety. Interacting with nature during the sunset can be a wonderful feeling. Here are some suggestions for connecting with nature at sunset and during twilight—or as I prefer, the Scottish term, *gloaming*—you feel a real sense of being between the worlds.

- At the seashore, throw flower petals into the surf and ask the blessings of Yemaya or another sea deity. Praise him or her and step into the surf sideways if you wish (as I mentioned before, it is considered rude to the deity just blunder on in full-frontal during a ritual act).
- In a wooded area, hug a tree or gather fallen leaves, acorns, pine cones, and so forth for your altar.
- In your own backyard, lie on your back on the ground and watch the sky turn colors and the stars come out. Wish upon the first star you see.

- By a pond or river try skipping stones and wishing on them. Take samples of natural waters wherever you find them at twilight—sweet or salt—for ritual and magickal use later on.

- Take your god and goddess statues or images outside during twilight to be blessed while "between the worlds" and to receive the simultaneous blessings of sunlight, starlight, and moonlight.

Eating a good meal while watching the sun's setting is always a sacred act; ever notice how "happy hour" begins around sunset? (Ever notice how many times I mention "happy hour" in this book?) Make it so by focusing on what you're eating and drinking. Eat slowly, savoring what you eat. Try not to eat heavy junk food or food laden with preservatives and lots of white flour and sugar at this time of day. If you must drink alcohol, savor a good wine, beer, or liqueur rather than one of those mixed drinks that are full of sugar, cream, or artificial color and flavor. If dining with others, enjoy conversation and try to refrain from complaining about the workday until after the sun has set. Share hugs and kisses with those you are dining with.

Many religious traditions—including ours—begin their holy days at sunset. This is a holdover from ancient times in which the day was measured from sunset to sunset. So if you get off work around 5 p.m. then, in reality, the day begins as yours to enjoy.

A Little Night Magick

Most of us do our magick at night. Why? Because it's spooky? Because it's harder for the neighbors to see what we're really doing?

Because we like to work with the moon's energy rather than the sun's? Well, yeah, but obviously, there are sound magickal reasons as well as the more irreverent ones just mentioned. And it's also usually the most convenient time to do so.

Also, many of us look to the moon for guidance as to what kind of magickal work to do. When the moon is waxing, do positive magick for increase, such as prosperity, fertility, love, and success. When the moon is waning, do banishing magick, getting rid of old problems, throwing off old "programming," cleansing yourself from toxic relationships, and so forth. Many folks have an esbat during the full moon, which many consider the most powerful time of the month. Others also have an esbat during the dark moon, even though some say this is a fallow time when it's probably best to not do magick at all. Still, there are several good books out there on dark moon magick, so someone must be doing something right at that time of month!

Speaking of "that time of the month," do you women honor your moontime? Well, I guess this is the old feminist in me, but I still honor my moontime by wearing red underwear (it's also more practical, if you know what I mean). Have you charted what phase the moon is in when you have your period? It might be a worthwhile endeavor. And though some Wiccans quail at the idea, it is perfectly appropriate to use menstrual fluid in certain rituals (during a Kali puja, for example). You might have to go to feminist Wiccan sources to find spells and rituals that utilize it, but they're out there. Just make sure that only the person whose blood it is touches it in order to be safe from even the slightest possibility of catching a blood-borne disease.

Speaking of moontime, do men have "periods"? Well, we now know that men have a menopause, although it is different from ours as men stay fertile beyond it. Still, if you are married or live with a man, try to chart his moods for a few months. Is there a pattern? Does a certain behavior or set of emotions surface during a particular phase of the moon? Hmm. Wonder if this has anything to do with the legends surrounding the werewolf myth. Isn't it interesting that most werewolves in the stories are male?

So maybe those guys who go out in the woods and drum (and who I usually laugh at) have a point after all. If men get in touch with their natural rhythms, perhaps it could help us all to get along better and understand each other a bit more.

Evening rites are as important as morning ones. A short guided meditation or "pure" meditation is best at night, for it helps calm one down from the day's jitters and relaxes one enough to encourage a sound sleep. Listening to a recording is a great way to meditate; choose some Hindu chants or songs, an Alan Watts tape, or a recording such as Joni Abbatecola's *Mistress of Dreams: A Dream Temple Journey*. Visit a well-stocked New Age store and peruse the tapes and CDs. The possibilities are endless.

Practice raising energy and grounding, cleanse and balance your chakras if need be, and shield yourself before retiring for the night (see Chapter 7). If you're exhausted and don't feel well, skip everything except the shielding and perhaps the Isis prayer. Don't forget to wish the deities goodnight, even if you only do so mentally.

Books such as *The Mysteries of Isis* give what are often called evening orisons for the deities. At night it is appropriate to thank the deities for a successful day before retiring. Many people also light candles and incense for their deities every evening—not a bad idea, and it's simple enough to do. After all, most of us have some sort of permanent altar in our homes. (I have several…they just keep multiplying.) Lighting a tea candle and the appropriate kind of incense is a very simple ritual that provides a good foundation for connection with one's chosen deity/deities.

Here is one of my own evening orisons to Thoth, the Egyptian god of the moon:

Awaken, Thoth

Em hotep, and em Ma'at,
In peace and in truth,
I celebrate your rising
In the night sky, o Thoth,
As your symbol, the moon.
In peace and in truth,
I absorb your wisdom
As I would moonlight,
Silvery and obscure,
Quiet and yet potent
As all secrets should be.
Arise, Thoth, arise
As we of magick honor thee
In peace, and in truth.

Now I'm thinking of a Blue Oyster Cult song called "I Love the Night." I think it's about a vampire or something, but it really is a love song to the night. Many of our kind know the feeling.

There's nothing like letting go of the day, changing out of that work "uniform," having a glass of wine, and letting the moonlight bathe you in its mysterious silvery magick. Turn off the lights and light the home with candles. Put on a meditation or visualization tape or, better yet, some sensuous dance music, and just glide around the room to the beat until you feel relaxed. Throw off your cares and do what you will for a while; the laundry and dishes can wait. This is YOUR time, it is OUR time, our magick time, and we should celebrate it.

A Prayer of Good-Night

May the lord and lady hold me
On this barque of sleep,
Where I float through moonlit
Lotus ponds and drink
The dew as glow-wine.
May I drift as a traveler
Through the mysteries of night
Through magick, through love,
Through sleep, into that open door
And back again, tomorrow.
Lord and Lady, guard my sleeping
Bones; my spirit rides
With Thee.

Now get some sleep!

Coda

Physician, Heal Thyself

"Coda" means "tail," and here's where the tail wags the dog. It was not an easy job writing this book. I wanted to be all sweetness and light (well, as much as I can be, anyway!) but, as the saying goes, life is what happens when you're making other plans. Other plans were in the works, clearly.

The days of physicians experimenting on themselves is not a memory. Alternative practitioners do it all the time, and even some allopathic doctors—especially those who have a theory that might not fit with conventional wisdom or the agendas of the drug companies—sometimes do it, too. As a "metaphysician" I, too, use myself as a test subject. Therefore, much of the material medica in this book had been tested on good ol' Dion-Isis.

And sometimes I am tested, too, by the powers that be. Sometimes it seems as though the more I try to help others in conjunction with my faith and my beliefs, the more the universe drops an Acme anvil on my head.

One of the members of my Iseum, Phillip Khonsu, reminded me that our faith is always being tested—especially when we try to exercise it! I had forgotten that. I suppose that each level of spirituality is tested in one way or another.

I won't bore you with the events that unfolded while I was writing this book. Suffice to say that the book got written in spite of it all, and for that I am doubly proud.

And that brings me to my main point: What are you proud of today? Is that a hard question? I'll bet it is. I'm proud that I had the self-control to not smack the guy who cut in line in front of me at Trader Joe's today. I'm proud that I went to acupuncture instead of having a cocktail after my not-very-good day was over.

Anyone who says that "pride goeth before a fall" is talking not about pride in the sense of self-esteem but rather hubris, which is another thing altogether. Hubris is from a Greek word, and what the Greeks were talking about was the kind of overconfidence that angers the gods. Pride is what we have when we take care of ourselves. It is a necessary component of being a successful human being.

If you couldn't think of anything right off the bat to be proud of, then I'd like to invite you to do the following chakra meditation exercise. In fact, why not do it anyway? If you've tried the chakra meditation in Chapter 7 then you're ready for this one. If not, then go back and work on that one first.

The Lotus Chakras

Start with obtaining small polished stones that match the colors of the chakras if you wish. You can place them at the appropriate parts of your body while lying on your back. Place the root chakra stone between your legs about mid-thigh, and place the crown chakra above your head so that it just touches the top of your head.

If you don't want to bother with the crystals you can, believe it or not, just get colored squares of construction paper; maybe some paper company makes Astrobright paper in the chakra shades. (If they don't then they should!)

We are going to work with the image of a lotus so you have to know what one looks like. Familiarize yourself with the blue lotuses as they are drawn by the Egyptians—they have spiky petals. Then familiarize yourself with the ones drawn by Asian artists—they have more rounded petals and are usually pink or red.

Once your crystals or color swatches are aligned and you can visualize the different types of lotuses, we will begin a bit differently than the previous meditation. This time, you will start at the crown chakra, and visualize it as a beautiful purple lotus blooming just above the crown of your head. Feel its sharp petals reaching toward the heavens. The petals pull in the energy of the cosmos, which you will bring down into your body.

Your next two chakras will also have the spiky waterlily petals, as they are often depicted in Egyptian art, and will be in deep blue and bright blue. With the heart chakra, the petals of the lotus now become more rounded and soft-looking, more similar to an Asian artistic rendering of a lotus.

Continue visualizing the lotuses in the appropriate chakra colors. When you get to the root chakra, feel the petals of the chakra saturating the ground and pulling up strength and grounding from the earth. Allow this stream to meld with the clear crystal stream from the heavens. With this you feel a sense of belonging, a sense of *rightness*, and a sense of completion. Know that you are a child of the earth and of the universe, and proudly so.

If possible, try to visualize a recent situation in which you were particularly proud of yourself. And when you are feeling good about yourself, open your eyes and put the stones or color swatches aside. Drink a glass of water, and go about your regular activities. Smile and hold your head high. Be proud.

Now I'm going to show you a way to shield yourself and love yourself simultaneously. This time you're going to shield yourself, as we did in Chapter 7, but with your arms crossed on your chest in "mummy" fashion. Place your palms on your chest and breathe deeply with your arms crossed in this way. Pat yourself and hug yourself while you visualize your shields. This way you are sending yourself both love and protection.

This is a lightweight book that just keeps getting heavier, so let's have some fun here! When I was a kid I loved waving sparklers around as though they were a magick wand on the 4th of July. Unfortunately, at least as far as sparklers are concerned, fireworks are no longer legal in my local area. But that doesn't mean we can't have a sparkler of a wand! Why not take whatever you use as a wand—be it a $500 gem-encrusted one from the New Age store or the one made of a straw with a cardboard-and-glitter star on the end that your child made (which would be the more magickal of the two, by the way)—and wave it around the room. Visualize a contrail of sparks as though the darn thing really threw them off! Pretend you're one of those cartoon characters who can wave a magick wand in this manner and just have fun with it. Consider this a quick way to clear the air around yourself. Do it often. And if sparklers are still available in your area, by all means use them as magick wands! But don't set anything on fire, okay?

Tut Tut, Stiff Upper Lip and All That, as the Brits Say

Believe me, I know just how hard it is to keep a stiff upper lip and stay strong about some things. I wish I could say that I could do that all the time. But I'd be lying, and then Thoth really would hit me on the knuckles with his ruler. So what do you do when you just feel as if you must have a "kick me" sign on your back? When you get home from work or school, do this:

Curl up in the fetal position in the room where you usually do your magick. We're not going to do this one outside, so if that's where you do magick, then do this one in your bedroom. Close your eyes and pretend to be a rock at the bottom of a stream. Imagine the water pouring over you, day in, day out. Do you feel stressed? Abused? Can't get any rest?

Now imagine that someone comes up to the stream. He or she is looking into the stream, and sees a beautiful stone. (What color is it?) The person (is it a god or goddess? An old prospector? A rockhound?) proclaims the beauty of the rock, how shiny it is, how lovely it is because the stream has tumbled it until it is smooth and beautiful and has no rough edges.

Now visualize yourself as beautiful, with no rough edges, all sophistication and sparkling wit and wisdom gained through a lifetime of experience. You see, the river hasn't worn you down—it's made you who you are, and you are beautiful.

If you wish to shut off the mind's eye television set now, then do so. Maybe you want to take a nap just the way you are. Maybe you want to curl up under the Wolfie blanket you got for Yule with your Anubis and Bastet stuffed toys (or maybe that's just me). Or perhaps you want to get up and get back to the world—standing a bit straighter than you were before we started, of course.

Test the affirmations and other suggestions in this book on yourself (and it's always fun to experiment on friends, too—if they're willing, that is!). Keep what works. Write notes in the margins and highlight the affirmations that work the best for you; dog-ear the pages. Write your own affirmations at the end of Appendix I. But bring yourself into yourself, then take yourself out into the world. Feel the exchange of energy wherever you go. Don't get too insulated, or too isolated. And most of all, Be Blesséd.

Appendix 1

Affirmations Express

Here's where I list what I consider to be the most important affirmations in the book, as a quick reference guide. (I'll leave some space for you to write in others as well!) Then I'll present some new affirmations that didn't seem to need a chapter all by themselves, but which might be just as useful as those that did.

Here are the affirmations I consider to be the most important ones in the book. Do these even if you don't do any of the rest of them.

I am beautiful and loved.

Isis attend me; Isis mend me.

I thank the god/dess for this day.

I am dust and water walking. (Lest you get too cocky!)

I believe in myself and my vision.

I stand in the light of the goddess.

The goddess hears my prayers.

My prayers are answered.

At work, the god/dess works through me.

I am a successful organism.

I am truly blessed by the gods.

Here's some space to add the ones you might like best that I haven't included here:

1. _____
2. _____
3. _____
4. _____
5. _____

Saying Grace

Many Wiccans and pagans do not say "grace" before a meal as it reminds them of unhappy associations with a previous unwanted spiritual path. Maybe one's tyrannical father made them say grace as a child or a relative slapped their hand if they started eating before grace was said. But we shouldn't let these unhappy memories keep us from giving thanks for our food, which is one of the most important reasons to thank the gods. Here are some suggestions:

Spend a moment of silence thinking about the abundance before you, even if it's a bologna sandwich and some potato chips. We as Americans have an embarrassment of riches when it comes to food. Here's what I'm thinking as I survey my meal:

"I was unhappy because I could not afford to go to Spago, until I met a man who couldn't afford McDonald's."

Well, maybe you're not as ironically minded as I am, but you get the idea.

Say a formal grace before a ritual or holiday feast, and especially on Thanksgiving:

We thank the Green Man and Lady Bountiful for this feast before us and ask that we may continue in their grace.

Don't forget to thank those earthly deities, either:

I thank you, Trader Joe's, for providing me with gourmet food at discount prices.

I thank my students for attending my classes and my readers for buying my books thus allowing me a livelihood so that I can provide for myself and enjoy a healthy diet.

I give thanks for the bounty of California, the state in which I am privileged to live.

I give thanks to Emperor Moctezuma, for sharing his chocolate with the rest of us.

Well, some of those may be kind of silly, but you get the idea. Now write some of your own:

1. _____
2. _____
3. _____
4. _____
5. _____

Especially for Men

Although I intend for both men and women to utilize this book, I will acknowledge that perhaps more women than men will use the affirmations. For example, not all men (at least not here in Western society) will feel comfortable affirming that "I am beautiful and loved." I have tried to include affirmations that seem to me to be "male-friendly," but of course I'm not sure how well I've done. It could be that I'm stereotyping in some way by including martial images such as those of the Horus falcon and suggesting affirmations aimed toward men that address issues of strength and courage to the exclusion of other virtues.

I thought I'd try a few out here and invite my male readers to see how they work. I'd appreciate any feedback, especially feedback that could set me in the right direction, if I've gone a bit off course. So here are a few affirmations I've written especially for the male of the species, although women, of course, can use them too:

I adapt and change as the Green Man changes throughout the seasons.

I am a part of nature and a co-creator of nature as is Cernunnos, Herne, (insert your favorite creator deity).

I am true to my vision and my God/dess.

Love comes naturally to me, as it did between the Goddess and the God.

❦

Like the Egyptian god Bes I honor my role as protector of children.

❦

I am a leader who leads through example, not iron.

❦

Red magick flows through me like the blood of Osiris.

(I'm riffing off a common Isian affirmation: "Red magick flows through me like the blood of Isis.")

And so on. I hope these will help all those dudes out there to use affirmations to improve themselves and their lives.

More Affirmations for the Working Day

May the firm find the funds to give us all raises.

❦

May our business prosper so that our employees and we prosper.

❦

May (insert name here) hire me as I am the best candidate for the job. (If you are the right person for the job, of course.)

❦

May the boss not see that e-mail I just sent to my sweetheart!

Today I will carry out my tasks with confidence and poise.

May the CEOs of the gods see that we need an IPO really soon!

I just noticed the other day at one of the colleges where I teach that an administrative assistant has a full-on altar at her workstation! It's not a pagan altar, although that's up for debate. It has angels, Mary, saints, and all kinds of good-luck charms. I guess it depends on the climate of the place you are working as to whether the powers that be would accommodate an altar of some type.

I also notice that many ethnic restaurants have altars of one sort or another, some prominently positioned and others more discreet. If you own your own business, I think it is in your best interests to have an altar somewhere on the premises. You can decide whether it's for the public to see or not.

Bless the Beasts and the Children

And everyone else, for that matter. You may have noticed that I mentioned more than once that I often extend my blessings, albeit most times silently, to others around me. There is nothing wrong with sending your blessings to others, even strangers. If they are not wanted or needed, then they will be ignored. And if they are appreciated, then the goodness you send will bounce back to you.

I admit that in a place with many others around me I feel silly if I ask for my own protection, for example, and ignore others. I mean, let's say I'm feeling that it's earthquake weather (no such thing, of course, just a rumor) and feel the need to shield myself from falling portions of overpasses and such. Should I ignore the others on the streets around me? Of course not. To do so seems to me to be another sort of hubris, and I wouldn't be a very good priestess or magickian if I acted that way.

And be gracious with others' blessings for yourself, as well. We may rankle at someone's assumption that we're Christian or Jewish or whatever, but if that someone is offering us a free blessing then, as with any other sort of door prize, I'm willing to take it. Remember that it is the intent that matters, not the pantheon in which it is robed. "Blessings to you, too, dear," might be an appropriate response.

Teach affirmations to kids. Even better: Have them make up their own. Kids have incredible magick because until they reach puberty no one tells them that magickal thinking is "wrong." As I told my Iseum at Imbolc, the most powerful wand I've ever had was made for me by the daughter of a friend. It was basically a stick with some feathers and a crystal or two glued onto it. I used it until it fell apart!

Speak affirmations to your pets—and to your garden and the creatures that dwell there as well. Remember all those experiments they did in the 1970s with music and plants? Well, if classical music helps them grow better, then maybe affirmations spoken to them will, too.

Affirmations and Spellcraft

Affirmations may be used as part of spells, and in and of themselves they are spells as well. When you speak or even think an affirmation, you are "affirming" the desire inherent in it; isn't that a spell? I think so. Perhaps we cannot distinguish between prayer, wish, and magick, because sometimes they seem so intertwined as to be the same thing.

Writing affirmations often makes them more similar to "spells" to people. Some like to write them on parchment with a special ink: so-called Dove's blood ink for love spells, some green ink for money spells, or Dragon's Blood ink for uncrossing. That's fine if you enjoy the trappings but, as I said previously, a cheap ballpoint and some recycled paper work just fine.

There is some truth to the idea of writing things down to make them more effective. I can, for instance, speak definitively about the benefits of taking notes in a class. Experiments have been done over and over again that prove that a class that takes notes—even if the students never reread their notes—will retain more material than the class that only listens. Listening and speaking are one thing; writing is another. Wise Thoth has told me to tell you that it is in the process of reading and writing that we distinguish ourselves from the "lower" animals. Yes, animals listen and speak in their own languages. But we amplify the intention of language by writing it down and then encouraging others to read what we have written. To read and to write are to perform strong magick; no wonder that those people whom society has wanted to take power away from—such as the slaves of early America or women in many parts of the world today—have been kept illiterate.

Certainly not all magick requires writing, and not all affirmations need to be written out. But if you want to use them to their best advantage, write them down. A psychotherapist will tell you, for example, that you should take those self-esteem affirmations and not just say them in front of the mirror but type them in large letters and then paste them onto the mirror as well! Posting words makes them laws, however, so beware of what you decide to write down and display.

One last affirmation:

I am loved by the God and the Goddess.

After all, thou art God/dess, and to love anyone else, you must first love yourself.

Know that you are loved.

Appendix II

Products and Services

Products

Aromatherapy

AuraCacia essential oils

www.auracacia.com

The most common brand of essential oils found in drugstores, health food stores and some supermarkets. Request a catalog on their Website.

Avalon Organics

www.avalonorganics.com

Organic lavender shower gel, hand soap, shampoo, etc. They have these same products with some other aromatherapy scents and unscented products. Very reasonably priced and excellent quality.

Soothe Your Soul
417 Pacific Coast Highway
Redondo Beach, CA 90277
(310) 798-8445

Fine aromatherapy products including their own blends; candles, incense, recordings, and books. Check your search engine; they should have a Website soon.

Candles

Root Candles
www.rootcandles.com
P.O. Box 706
Medina, OH 44256
(800) 768-3394

Fine scented candles. Currently the only major American candle company making black, patchouli-scented candles. They also offer saints' candles and other liturgical candles, including custom orders.

Yankee Candle
www.yankeecandle.com

Fine scented candles; you can find appropriate scents and colors for most seasonal occasions; some are naturally scented. Use the "Store Locator" feature on the Website to find a store near you.

Magickal Supplies

Beyond Physical
Connie Jones
www.beyondphysical.com

Connie is a member of the Iseum and makes handmade soap, including the ritual hyssop soap mentioned, and other bath products, candles, teas, etc.

Dragonmarsh
www.dragonmarsh.com
3744 Main St.
Riverside, CA 92501
(951) 276-1116

Pretty good selection of fresh herbs as well as magickal bath products, Renaissance Faire supplies, fabrics, candles, etc. You might see them at a Southern California fair or pagan gathering.

Indio Products
www.indioproducts.com
236 W. Manchester Ave.
Los Angeles, CA 90003
(323) 778-2233/(800) 944-1414

Think of them as your supermarket warehouse store for all things magickal—caters primarily to followers of Voodoo, Hoodoo, Santeria, and related paths. Their Los Angeles warehouse store is highly recommended.

Raven's Flight

www.ravensflight.net

(888) 84-RAVEN

Though Raven no longer has a brick-and-mortar store, her products are still available online and at pagan festivals throughout Southern California. Her ritual blends are highly recommended; my favorite is Before the Rite Shower Gel.

Sacred Source

www.sacredsource.com

P.O. Box 163WW

Crozet, VA 22932

(800) 290-6203

The best source for statues and images of deities from a variety of cultures. Available online and as a print catalog.

Organic Food and Hard-to-Find Grocery Items

Bristol Farms

www.bristolfarms.com/locations/index.html

High-end supermarkets where you can find unusual imported items and exotic fruits, vegetables, and liquors.

Trader Joe's

www.traderjoes.com

Upscale bargain purveyors of wine, cheese, and some organic products, including toiletries.

Whole Foods

www.wholefood.com/stores/index.html

Expensive "health food" chain stores with much organic food and a good selection of supplements and aromatherapy products.

Recordings and Videos/DVDs

Mystic Fire Videos

www.mysticfire.com

A good source for Alan Watts, Maya Deren, and other classics of metaphysics, the mysterious, and the avant garde.

Sequoia Records

www.sequoiarecords.com

P.O. Box 280

Topanga, CA 90290

Producers of New Age and Wiccan/pagan recording artists.

Recommended: *Beneath the Veil,* and *Dancers of Twilight,* by Zingaia; *Fairy HeartMagic, Fairy Night Songs,* and *Fairy of the Woods,* by Gary Stadler.

White Swan Music

www.whiteswanmusic.com

New Age and related styles of music.

Recommended: *Love is Space* and *Satsang,* by Deva Primal and Miten.

Teas

Chanakara Teas

www.chanakara.com

Teas for all your chakras! You can buy a box of a single tea/chakra or an assortment of all seven. These are made by the Stash Tea company of Oregon. Ask for a catalog.

Floradix

Salus-Haus

Made in Germany/Distributed in the U.S. by Flora, Inc.

Lynden, WA 98264

One of the first lines of European tisanes exported to the United States. Many of their teas are fine for rituals and many are organic, such as their Vervain tea. Check stores that cater to Europeans; the first places I ever bought herb teas, long before they were popular outside of Craft circles, were the herb stores of Alpine Village in Torrance, CA.

TenRen Tea

www.tenren.com

Makers of Ti Kwan Yin and other fine Asian teas with stores in San Francisco, Los Angeles, New York, Toronto, Chicago, and Vancouver. I highly recommend a trip to their stores in Los Angeles's Chinatown and especially the store that is their home base in San Francisco's Chinatown. It's really amazing.

Vintage Tea Leaf
www.VintageTeaLeaf.com
969 Broadway
Long Beach, CA 90802
(562) 435-5589

My Iseum loves their Black Lotus Royal tea—the finest lotus tea I've ever found. They have an amazing assortment, and if you're in the L.A. area it's well worth a trip to their tea room.

Services

Isian/Pagan/Wiccan and Other Spiritual Organizations Mentioned in This Book and/or Recommended

The Fellowship of Isis
Lady Olivia Robertson
Clonegal Castle
Enniscorthy, Eire

The parent organization for the Iseums, Lyceums, and Egyptian Temples listed. Founded by Lady Olivia Robertson and her brother and sister-in-law in the 1970s, The Fellowship continues to be the premier organization for Isian and eclectic Wiccans and pagans.

The Goddess Temple of Orange County
Rev. Ava Park, Founder
www.goddesstempleoforangecounty.com
17905 Sky Park Circle
Suite A
Irvine, CA 92614
(949) 651-0564

As if founding a Goddess Temple in Orange County weren't amazing enough, founder Ava Park has also made it a women's sanctuary. Though some of the events are open to men as well as women, the Sunday services and most of the events are for women and girls only.

Hygeia's Bowl Healing Arts
Laura Sedgwick, M.S. Lic. A.
Hygeia@hygeiasbowl.com

Laura is a wonderful acupuncturist and also works with chakras, Chinese herbs, and aromatherapy. She understands the viewpoint of Wiccan and pagan clients and can serve them particularly well.

The Iseum of Isis Paedusis
Reverends Dion-Isis, Nyx, and Stephania, Priestesses
Isis_Paedusis@hotmail.com
P.O. Box 83
Manhattan Beach, CA 90267-0083

The Iseum of myself and my two co-priestesses. We celebrate the major sabbats for interested parties in the South Bay regions of Los Angeles County and also offer talks and events led by prominent pagan authors and practicioners.

Isis Ancient Cultures and Religion Society (IACRS)

Rev. Karen Tate, Heirophant

home.earthlink.net/~specialjourn

IACRS@comcast.net

The priestesses of the Iseum of Isis Paedusis were ordained by Rev. Karen Tate. She presents occasional rituals as well as special occasion lectures, films, slides, and events. Under A Special Journey Travel she presents tours to sacred sites around the world. Her new book, *Sacred Places of Goddess: 108 Destinations* (San Francisco: Consortium of Collective Consciousness, 2006) is now available.

Isis Oasis—Home of the Temple of Isis

Right Reverend Loreon Vigne

www.isisoasis.org

20889 Geyserville Ave.

Geyserville, CA 95441

(800) 679-7387

Rev. Vigne hosts the Convocation each year for groups allied under the banner of the Fellowship of Isis. Most of us who are legally ordained as Isian ministers in California are registered as such by her organization. The Oasis is also a wonderful place to have a retreat near California's wine country. In addition, she runs an ocelot sanctuary!

Long Beach Womanspirit

www.longbeachwomanspirit.org

Well-known for their Winter and Summer faires, this group often pairs with The Temple of Isis Los Angeles for seasonal rituals, usually in the Long Beach, CA, area.

Temple Eclectica
Melody Friend, Facilitator
maddiesmelody@yahoo.com

Truly an eclectic temple. Melody holds seasonal sabbats, Native American ceremonies, and Buddhist and Hindu rituals, including a once-a-week meditation session. E-mail for current events or to book your own event.

The Temple of Goddess Spirituality Dedicated to Sekhmet
Genevieve Vaughan, Founder
www.sekhmettemple.com
P.O. Box 94
Indian Springs, NV 89018
(702) 524-9995

This fascinating retreat in Nevada is about 40 miles north of Las Vegas. Some of the accommodations are for men and women; some are women-only. They hold political protests, Egyptian rituals, and Native American rituals by the local Shoshone tribe.

Temple of Isis Los Angeles
Rev. Laura Janesdaughter, Heirophant
www.toila.com

One of the premier local Isian/eclectic groups; the Iseum of Isis Paedusis was chartered by the Temple of Isis Los Angeles.

Appendix III

References

Abbatecola, Joni, Ph.D. *Lady of the Lotus*. CD. Studio City, Calif.: 2000.

———. *Mistress of Dreams*. CD. Studio City, Calif.: 2000.

Arcaute, Francisco. Personal interview.

Ardinger, Barbara, Ph.D. *Practicing the Presence of the Goddess*. Novato, Calif.: New World Library, 2000.

Bisson, Terry. *Bears Discover Fire*. New York: Tor, 1993.

Breasted, James H. *Development of Religion and Thought in Ancient Egypt*. Philadelphia: University of Pennsylvania Press, 1972.

Budge, E. A. Wallis. *The Egyptian Book of the Dead*. New York: Dover, 1967.

Butler, W. E. *How to Read the Aura and Practice Psychometry, Telepathy, & Clairvoyance*. Rochester, Vt.: Destiny Books, 1998.

Cabot, Laurie, with Tom Cowan. *Power of the Witch*. New York: Dell, 1989.

Carter, Karen Rauch. *Move Your Stuff, Change Your Life*. New York: Fireside, 2000.

Cousins, Norman. *Anatomy of an Illness*. New York: Norton & Company, 1979.

Davies, Brenda, Ph.D. *The Seven Healing Chakras*. Berkeley, Calif.: Ulysses Press, 2000.

———. *Unlocking the Heart Chakra*. Berkeley, Calif.: Ulysses Press, 2001.

Dumars, Denise and Lori Nyx. *The Dark Archetype*. Franklin Lakes, N.J.: New Page Books, 2003.

Ebony, Stephania. Personal interview.

Ellis, Normandi. *Awakening Osiris: The Egyptian Book of the Dead*. Grand Rapids, Mich.: Phanes Press, 1988.

———. *Feasts of Light: Celebrations for the Seasons of Life Based on the Egyptian Goddess Mysteries*. Wheaton, Ill.: Quest Books, 1999.

Friend, Melody. Personal interview.

Gawain, Shakti. *Creative Visualization*. New York: Bantam, 1982.

Helgason, Jeff. Personal interview.

Jones, Connie. Personal interview.

Kushner, Harold S. *When Bad Things Happen to Good People.* New York: Shocken Books, 1981.

Maurine, Camille, and Lorin Roche, Ph.D. *Meditation Secrets for Women.* New York: HarperCollins, 2001.

McGarey, William A., M.D. *The Edgar Cayce Remedies.* New York: Bantam, 1983.

Mishlove, Jeffrey. *The Roots of Consciousness: Psychic Liberation Through History, Science and Experience.* New York: Random House, 1975.

Morrison, Dorothy. *Enchantments of the Heart: A Magical Guide to Finding the Love of Your Life.* Franklin Lakes, N.J.: New Page Books, 2002.

Moura, Ann. *Green Witchcraft II: Balancing Light and Shadow.* St. Paul, Minn.: Llewellyn, 1999.

Nyx, Lori. Personal interview.

Peck, M. Scott, M.D. *The Road Less Traveled and Beyond.* New York: Touchstone, 1999.

Perricone, Nicholas, M.D. *The Acne Prescription.* New York: HarperCollins, 2003.

Premal, Deva & Miten. *Love Is Space.* CD. Boulder, Colo.: White Swan Music, 2000.

———. *Satsang.* CD. Boulder, Colo.: White Swan Music, 2002.

Regula, deTraci. *The Mysteries of Isis.* St. Paul, Minn.: Llewellyn, 2002.

Roderick, Timothy. *The Once Unknown Familiar.* St. Paul, Minn.: Llewellyn, 1994.

Rollin, Betty. *First, You Cry*. New York: HarperCollins, 2000.

Scully, Nicki. *The Golden Cauldron: Shamanic Journeys of the Path of Wisdom*. Santa Fe, N.M.: Bear & Company, 1991.

Sedgwick, Laura, M.S., L. Ac. Personal interview.

Silverwind, Selene. *Magic for Lovers*. Berkeley, Calif.: Crossing Press, 2003.

Sylvan, Dianne. *The Circle Within*. St. Paul, Minn.: Llewellyn, 2004.

Weil, Andrew, M.D. *Eight Weeks to Optimum Health*. New York: Knopf, 1997.

Williams, David, M.D. Personal interview.

Index

A
Abbatecola, Joni, 185
ACLU, 38
Adult Attention Deficit
    Disorder, 60
Adventures of Hercules, The, 67
affirmations for
    a good night, 177
    arising, 15
    auto protection, 26
    beasts, 201
    being here now, 51
    children, 201
    express, 195
    mindfulness, 51
    self-esteem for life, 31
    sickness and health, 113
    talking to a god, 63
    work, 99
    working day, the, 200
African/Afro-Caribbean Gods, 70
air travel, 28
Andrews, Julie, 67
Anubis, 132, 177
Apollo, 15
Ardinger, Dr. Barbara, 13
Asian/Pacific Gods, 70
astral familiar, 148
Athena, 26
Awakening Osiris, 16

B
balancing chakras, 170
bamboo, 46-47
barter, 123

Bassett, Angela, 69
Beaumont, Charles, 34
Big Lebowksi, The, 69
Bisson, Terry, 128
Book of Coming Forth by Day, The, 16
book of shadows, 158
Brandon, Richard, 67
breast cancer, 181
Bridges, Jeff, 69
Buddhism, 12
Buffy the Vampire Slayer, 67, 109
Burberry, 41
Butler, W.E., 124

C

Candomble, 64
Carter, Karen Rauch, 165
CEOs/generals, 67
chakras, the lotus, 191
Chan, Jackie, 69
chi gong stretches, 16-18
Christian devil, 103
Christianity, 12, 64
Circle Within, The, 129
clearing chakras, 170
Crosby, Bing, 69
Crying Child Syndrome, 62

D

daily devotions, 12
Dark Archetype, The, 106
Davies, Dr. Brenda, 163
dialogues with deities, 63
diet, eat a balanced, 39
domovoy, 150
Dudes, 69
dying with dignity, 119

E

Ebony, Stephania, 12, 160
Egyptian Book of the Dead, The, 16
Egyptian Djed pillar, 45-46
Egyptian/Middles Eastern Gods, 70
Elephant Man, the, 36
Enchantments of the Heart, 161
energy beach ball, 143
everyday magick, 129

F

familiar
    friends, 147
    astral, 148
    meeting your, 151
feeling the situation, 60
feng shui, 165-166
fibromyalgia, 137
Franklin, Benjamin, 125
Friend, Melody, 17, 53

G

gloaming, 182
Gods, types of, 70
grace, saying, 197
Greek/Roman Gods, 70
greeting
    the gods, 22
    the sun, 15
grimoire, 158
group marriage, 162
guided visualizations, 71

H

Hecate, 68
Helios, Rise, 24
Hindo, 65

Index

Hindu/Tibetan Gods, 70
homeopath, 114
Hoodoo, 108
Hope, Bob, 69
How to Read the Aura, 124
hubris, 190

I
ibis, 66
Isis Prayer, The, 20, 117, 120-122
Islam, 12, 64

J
Judaism, 12, 64
June gloom, 23

K
Kali Yuga, 117
Keys, Alicia, 12
Khonsu, Phillip, 190

L
Liddy, G. Gordon, 131
love magick, 160
Lynch, David, 36

M
Ma'at, 107
Mabon, 182
Macy's, 41
Magic for Lovers: Creating Lasting Love with Wicca Spells and Tantric Techniques, 161
magick for the whole family, 141
magickal talents, 174
marijuana, 119-120
Mask, 36

meditation, write your own, 90
men, especially for, 198
mindfulness over matter spell, 62
misogynist, 115
Mistress of Dreams, A Dream Temple Journey, 185
morning prayer, 16
Mount Olympus, 68
Move Your Stuff, Change Your Life, 165
Murphy, Eddie, 69
Mysteries of Isis, The, 19, 185

N
Native American/Mesoamerican Gods, 70
New York Public Library, 34
Nordstrom, 41
Norse pantheon, 27
Norse/Celtic/Slavic Gods, 70

O
Once Unknown Familiar, The, 150, 153
Osiris, 16, 45
Oya, 106

P
Papa Legba, 85
Perricone, Dr. Nicholas, 41
Pilates, 18
Poitier, Sydney, 67
polyamory, 161
pranic breathing
  exercises, 24
  instructions, 54-55
prayers, for self-esteem, 33

praying to idols, 64
priorities, sense of appropriate, 59
professors, 68

Q
Quinn, Anthony, 67

R
Ragnarok, 179
recipes for success, 111
Regula, deTraci, 19
reverent irreverence, 65
Ritalin, 60
ritual bathing, 19
Roderick, Timothy, 150
Russian folklore, 150

S
Samhain, 131
Santeria, 64-65
scrapbooking, 158-160
scrying safely, 144
Seasonal Affective Disorder, 23
seasonal pagans, 11
Sekhmet of the Sun, 22
self-esteem
    for life, 31
    spell, 47
Sephora, 41
7 Healing Chakras, The,
    163, 170
Sex in the City, 69
shielding, 142
Shiva, 117-119
Silverwinds, Selene, 161
Smile, 36
sonrisa, 37
Sound of Music, The, 67

spirituality, practicing, 12
Stuart, Gloria, 68
Sylvan, Dianne, 129

T
Tai Chi, 18
Temple Eclectica, 17, 53
Thelma and Louise, 69
They're Made of Meat, 128
time of troubles, 117
To Sir, With Love, 67
travel protection, 26
Trump, Donald, 67
Twilight Zone, The, 34
twilight, 178

U
Unlocking the Heart Chakra, 163

V
Vanishing American, the, 34
Vigoda, Abe, 68
visualization
    practicing, 151
    lotus, 192
    with Dhambala, 84-90
    with Kwan Yin, 78-84
    with Thor, 72-78
voudou, 64

W
Waiting to Exhale, 69
Watts, Alan, 54
weight issues, 44
wife swapping, 162
Williams, Dr. David, 132
womb-man, 115

Y
Yemata, 65

About the Author

Rev. Denise "Dion-Isis" Dumars, M.A., is a college instructor and writer who lives in the beautiful South Bay area of Los Angeles. She has taught English composition, literature, and creative writing at many local colleges and universities, including such prestigious institutions as Pepperdine University's Seaver College and Antioch University Los Angeles. She has published numerous poems, short stories, reviews, interviews, travel articles, and all manner of entertainment journalism. She has even had a screenplay optioned—proving that she is, indeed, a native Californian. This is her third full-length book.

In addition to teaching and writing she enjoys public speaking on metaphysical topics and often lectures at bookstores and metaphysical and New Age venues. She also works as a creativity consultant and has developed a very popular creative writing class taught entirely within sacred space, called Writing from the Sacred Source, or, The Goddess is my Co-Writer. She is currently forming writing workshops, Salons of Seshet, in Southern California. Her course is only available to private groups as no institute of higher learning has so far allowed her to teach it!

She is a legally ordained minister in the Temple of Isis/Fellowship of Isis and is a Priestess of Isis, Thoth, and Yemaya and is co-founder of the Iseum of Isis Paedusis. When not working (which isn't very often) she enjoys traveling to such exotic locales as Mexico, Canada, France, England, and—that holy land—Las Vegas.